ABRAHAM'S
JOURNEY

MeOtzar HoRav SERIES:

SELECTED WRITINGS OF RABBI JOSEPH B. SOLOVEITCHIK

The *Me-Otzar HoRav* series has been made possible
by a generous grant from Ruth and Irwin Shapiro.

The publication of *Abraham's Journey*
has been made possible by a grant from
Julius and Dorothy Berman
in memory of his parents
Rabbi Henoch and Sarah D. Berman.

ABRAHAM'S JOURNEY

Reflections on the Life
of the Founding Patriarch

Rabbi Joseph B. Soloveitchik

Edited by
David Shatz, Joel B. Wolowelsky, and Reuven Ziegler

Published for
TORAS HORAV FOUNDATION
by KTAV Publishing House

ABRAHAM'S JOURNEY
REFLECTIONS ON THE LIFE OF THE FOUNDING PATRIARCH
Rabbi Joseph B. Soloveitchik
Edited by David Shatz, Joel B. Wolowelsky, and Reuven Ziegler

© 2008 TORAS HORAV FOUNDATION
This material is protected by copyright and may not be reproduced in any form, including translation, without permission in writing from the
TORAS HORAV FOUNDATION, 425 Park Avenue, Suite 970, New York, NY 10022

Library of Congress Cataloging-in-Publication Data

Soloveitchik, Joseph B.
   Abraham's journey : reflections on the life of the founding patriarch
/ Joseph B. Soloveitchik ; edited by David Shatz, Joel B. Wolowelsky,
and Reuven Ziegler.
      p. cm. -- (Meotzar horav series ; 9)
   ISBN 978-1-60280-004-5
   1. Abraham (Biblical patriarch) 2. Bible. O.T. Genesis--Criticism,
interpretation, etc. I. Shatz, David. II. Wolowelsky, Joel B. III.
Ziegler, Reuven. IV. Title.
   BS580.A3S55 2008
   222'.11092
                              2007045660

Printing year: 2021

ISBN 978-1-60280-004-5

Published for
THE TORAS HORAV FOUNDATION by

KTAV PUBLISHING HOUSE
527 Empire Blvd.
Brooklyn, NY 11225

Website: www.ktav.com
Email: orders@ktav.com
ph: (718)972-5449 / Fax: (718)972-6307

ME-OTZAR HORAV SERIES:
SELECTED WRITINGS OF RABBI JOSEPH B. SOLOVEITCHIK

EDITORIAL-PUBLICATION BOARD
David Shatz, Series Editor
Joel B. Wolowelsky, Associate Editor
Reuven Ziegler, Director of Research

Volume One
Family Redeemed
Edited by David Shatz and Joel B. Wolowelsky

Volume Two
Worship of the Heart
Edited by Shalom Carmy

Volume Three
Out of the Whirlwind
Edited by David Shatz, Joel B. Wolowelsky, and Reuven Ziegler

Volume Four
Community, Covenant, and Commitment
Edited by Nathaniel Helfgot

Volume Five
The Emergence of Ethical Man
Edited by Michael Berger

Volume Six
Festival of Freedom
Edited by Joel B. Wolowelsky and Reuven Ziegler

Volume Seven
The Lord Is Righteous in All His Ways
Edited by Jacob J. Schacter

Volume Eight
Days of Deliverance
Edited by Eli D. Clark, Joel B. Wolowelsky, and Reuven Ziegler

Volume Nine
Abraham's Journey
Edited by David Shatz, Joel B. Wolowelsky, and Reuven Ziegler

• Table of Contents •

• Preface •

*A*braham's Journey: Reflections on the Life of the Founding *Patriarch* is the ninth volume of the series *MeOtzar HoRav: Selected Writings of Rabbi Joseph B. Soloveitchik*. Rabbi Soloveitchik *zt"l* (1903-1993) was one of the outstanding talmudists of the twentieth century, and one of its most creative and seminal Jewish thinkers. "The Rav," as he is widely known, brought Jewish thought and law to bear on the interpretation and assessment of the modern experience. He built bridges between Judaism and the modern world while vigorously upholding the integrity and autonomy of the Jew's faith commitment, in particular the commitment to a life governed by Halakhah, Jewish law.

For over four decades, Rabbi Soloveitchik gave the senior *sh'iur* (class in Talmud) at the Rabbi Isaac Elchanan Theological Seminary (RIETS), affiliated with Yeshiva University. Generations of rabbinical students were taught and inspired by him, among them many of the future leaders of all areas of Jewish communal life. He was the halakhic authority and spiritual leader of the Rabbinical Council of America, founded the Maimonides School in Boston, and also served as the chief rabbinic figure in that city (commuting weekly between there and New York). He contributed vitally to the dynamic resurgence of Orthodox Judaism in America.

Although many of Rabbi Soloveitchik's writings and discourses have been published over the years, much additional material remains in handwritten manuscripts and tapes. The Toras HoRav Foundation was established by family members and former students to disseminate these and other works, with the aim of enhancing both our grasp of Rabbi Soloveitchik's philosophy and our understanding of the diverse topics he addressed.

This volume presents the Rav's reflections on Abraham, the founding patriarch of the Jewish people. We hope that by experiencing the Rav's rare blend of intellectual sweep and energizing passion, the reader will find the Rav's thought an invaluable and integral part of his or her own spiritual quest.

David Shatz
Joel B. Wolowelsky
Reuven Ziegler

❧ *Introduction*

The present volume focuses on the life of *Avraham Avinu*, founding patriarch of the Jewish People. As we encounter Rabbi Soloveitchik's analyses of the various themes and episodes of the Abraham narratives in Genesis, we should keep in mind how the Rav characterizes his method:

> Besides our understanding of the semantics of the words, their style, and the historical background, there is a great spiritual message, a *kerygma*. The Torah is not concerned exclusively with past events; it is also concerned with our thoughts, our feelings, and our commitments. . . This is certainly true of the first book of the Bible. Human destiny is reflected in Genesis—human triumph and defeat, human greatness and smallness, the potential of what man is capable of achieving, his opportunities and even his defiance of the Master of the Universe

Through careful exegesis of verses, illuminating analyses of character, and insightful readings of *midrashim* and classic medieval commentators, the essays in this book seek the *kerygma* of the Abraham story.

A central goal of the study of Abraham is to build out of his actions and qualities a theory of the human being, a religious anthropology, an understanding of the human being's relationship with God. Moreover, the Abraham narratives teach us about past and present events in the life of the Jewish people:

> When we speak about Abraham, we must always remember that the Bible is not only a book narrating events that transpired so many millennia ago. It speaks of events that are still taking place before our eyes. Actually, it is a book not only of Abraham but also of the destiny of our people. We are an eternal people, and our destiny is eternal—and the *Humash* is the book of our destiny.

Here the Rav applies a Nahmanidean principle often expressed in paraphrase as *"ma'aseh avot siman la-banim,* the events involving the fathers are signs for their descendants." Abraham is not only the first Jew, but also a historical prototype, his experiences and actions foreshadowing critical patterns in the history of his people. In a striking turn, the Rav interprets *"siman"* as indicative not of historical determinism, but of human free choice, namely, the responsibility to interpret events in a proper fashion so as to learn from them.

In addition to being a historical prototype, Abraham serves as a spiritual and ethical model. He questioned the status quo of his society and searched for God. He obeyed divine commands unhesitatingly, even when they entailed exile and sacrifice. He was drawn to the holy, departing his birthplace for an unknown destination and identifying the sacred land himself.

In consonance with the Rav's emphasis on the imperative of joining the *masorah,* the chain of interpretive tradition, the essays in this volume draw upon midrashic and other traditional sources in constructing their vivid portraits of Abraham and other biblical figures. For example, the discussion of Abraham's discovery of God is based on Maimonides' presentation, which includes a particular reconstruction of midrashic texts; Abraham's discovery is nowhere recorded in the Bible. These essays similarly bring alive such personalities as Abraham's father Terah, his nephew Lot, his wife Sarah, and even obscure figures such as Melchizedek king of Salem. We learn from their deeds, their character, and their relationships to Abraham, who was both a social being and a solitary friend of God.

Abraham was a wanderer, a teacher, a lonely iconoclast, a master of sacrifice, a knight of faith and a stranger yet resident in his host society, a *ger ve-toshav*. He was *"Avraham ha-Ivri"*— the Jew who, in the image of the Midrash, stands on one side, while the rest of the world stands on the other (*"Ivri"* derived from *"ever,"* connoting "on the other side"). Indeed, the Rav reminds us, "To become a Jew has meant to be alienated from the rest of society. The destiny of *Avraham ha-Ivri*, the lonely Abraham, has always accompanied the Jew."

Abraham's *hesed* or loving-kindness (expressed most famously through *hakhnasat orehim*, the welcoming of guests) provides paradigms for how Jews should conduct themselves in the many and varied circumstances they confront. Likewise, Abraham's activity as a teacher—itself an instance of *hesed*—establishes pedagogy as a central value in Jewish life. The imperative of teaching flows not just from *hesed*, but from true scholarship and knowledge of God:

> To know God also means to have a desire to share one's knowledge with others, to have a longing to teach people, to bring the message to the ignorant and insensitive or to those unfortunate ones who have not had the opportunity to learn and to study. A man who is happy and does not want to teach others is not necessarily cruel and selfish. But he is not a scholar. A real scholar cannot contain what he knows within himself; he explodes. Knowledge entails a dynamic element; the knower

becomes restless, the truth cries out from the inner recesses of his personality, and he must tell others.

In this heartfelt passage, the Rav emerges as a true student of Abraham, and we continue to benefit from his emulation of the first Jewish teacher.

* * *

The core of this volume is taken from the Rav's Saturday night classes held at his Maimonides School, particularly from a series of more than twenty lectures on *parashat Lekh Lekha* given between October 1968 and April 1969, two series of lectures on the first chapter of Maimonides' *Hilkhot Avodat Kokhavim* in 1973 and in 1974, and classes on the relevant Torah portions extending throughout the 1970's. However, he also spoke about *Avraham Avinu* at various other venues, such as the third year of his seminar on "Judaism's Conception of Man" to an interdenominational group of rabbis in 1959-1960 and addresses to Yeshiva University Rabbinic Alumni in 1968 and 1973. These, too, have been incorporated into this volume. Each talk would contain a new insight, even when he was simply reviewing the previous week's *shi'ur* as an introduction. Nevertheless, portions of the various talks overlapped, and the editors, in collecting the material, arranged the Rav's words by topic and eliminated, whenever possible, repetition of ideas. Most of this material was available to the editors in the Rav's original manuscripts, a number of which could not be dated, and the rest was filled in with tape transcripts. The editors provided the headings for the chapters and subsections as well as the title of the volume.

Three chapters published in earlier volumes of the *MeOtzar HoRav* series relate to Abraham and are not included here: "Parenthood: Natural and Redeemed" in *Family Redeemed*; "Abraham Mourns Sarah" in *Out of the Whirlwind*; and "The

Charismatic Personality: Abraham" in *The Emergence of Ethical Man.*

Many people contributed to the production of this volume. We thank Yaakov Beasley, Doron Friedlander and Nadine Gesundheit for their valuable work on various aspects of the book; Marc Herman, Sholem Hurwitz, and Dov Karoll for checking the sources; Robert Milch for copy editing; Dimitri Y. Milch for proofreading; and Rachael Gelfman for preparing the index. We also thank Abraham Levovitz *z"l* for having provided a number of tapes. Several rabbis, educators, and laypersons were generous in sharing their expertise with us, and it is a pleasure to extend thanks to them as well: Daniel Frank, Abraham Kurtz, Aryeh Lieberman, Menachem Meier, Jacob J. Schacter, Avigdor Shinan, Avi Shmidman, Josef Stern, and Avner Taler. Yair Kahn reviewed the manuscript and provided valuable comments.

We extend our continued appreciation to the Toras HoRav Foundation for affording us the opportunity to further bring the Rav's Torah to a long-awaiting public. We are most grateful to Rabbi Aharon and Dr. Tovah Lichtenstein for their continued guidance during the editing process and for reviewing our work at various stages, including the final manuscript.

Abraham courageously revolutionized human thinking and initiated our covenantal relationship with God. Yet, the Rav notes, Jews share in the universal historical experience as members of humanity and must contribute to the general welfare of mankind. May these essays help us all appreciate that— in the book's closing words—"to experience this tension is precisely what it means to be an elected community, the descendants of Abraham."

❧ Abraham as Personality and Paradigm

Experiencing History

To write about Abraham today would appear to be a peculiar, if not absurd, undertaking. How can an ancient figure, enveloped in the fog of mystery and (in the opinion of today's cynical man) myth, fascinate the imagination and vision of modern scholars or preachers? They confront innumerable problems of enormous magnitude and force, and face situations which captivate their fantasy with both greatness and perplexing tragedy. Why should they investigate and probe a person who emerges from the unknown historic twilight, whose contours and features are blurred and almost imperceptible to the onlooker, while there is a world full of marvels, light, and charm that wink at and tantalize us? Why watch a bubble riding on the crest of a wave disappearing at the distant horizon, while a mighty tide rolls on toward us and breaks at our feet?

The historian will say that Abraham cannot be considered an archaeological reality, since, measured by the conventional standards of historical evidence, we cannot assert as a certainty that such a person lived and acted in the way the Bible describes. Many a Bible critic, Jew or gentile, casts serious doubt upon the authenticity of the narrative about this strange and unique man. No inscriptions or other pieces of documentary evidence have been discovered that mention even once the name of the patriarch. Perhaps Abraham is nothing but a myth, a legend, a vision of a tribe or a clan that assigned to its progenitor the role of God's fellow-companion and recorded out of this fantasy the dialogues and arguments, tribulations and joyous moments, of that imaginary figure.

As a matter of fact, this sort of skepticism regarding the biblico-historical accounts has, of late, lost much of its vigor and arrogance. Recent excavations and discoveries have confirmed many biblical accounts—not only in their general outlines but, more important, in their minute details, such as names of geographic places, travel routes, and cultic forms. Historians have begun to look upon the Bible as a book replete with historically true records. Excavations in the Negev have unearthed a rich civilization reminiscent of the biblical narratives concerning the economic and cultural surroundings in which Abraham lived and worked. In a word, the fury of the historian—the passionate seeker of truth—against the "Abraham myth" has abated. One will think twice nowadays before denying the existence of such a person.

To us, this problem is almost irrelevant. We need no evidence of the historical existence of our patriarch, just as there is no necessity for clear-cut logical evidence concerning the reality of God. The immediacy and aboriginal impact of our God-experience, cutting through all levels of existence and forming the very essence of our ontic awareness, does not require any other form of evidence and is not subject to logico-deductive or inductive verification. The latter is dependent upon a postulate-premise, whereas the God-experience is prior to cognitive activities of every kind, including the act of postulation. We may deal in a similar manner with the historical "proofs" of the existence of Abraham. As the architect and founder of our nation,

Abraham left such an indelible imprint upon our unfolding historic destiny that he has been integrated into our historical consciousness; he is so singular a motif of our historical emergence that the whole paradoxical, complex experience of our charisma would be impossible if we denied the reality of the Abraham-personality. The narrative about his life is almost, to use a Kantian term, an apodictic truth, a constitutive category that activates our great historical experience and lends it meaning and worth. If we were to deny the truth of the Abraham story, our historic march would be a fathomless mystery, an insensate, cruel, absurd occurrence that prosecutes no goal and moves on toward nothingness, running down to its own doom. The great figure of our patriarch is indispensable because it suggests a meaning and an end that are within the grasp of historical realization. The axiological character of our historical process can be determined only in relation to the figure of Abraham. If Abraham were a myth, a legend, a beautiful but fantastic vision, then we would be faced with a tragic hoax and the ridicule of the centuries and millennia.

The old problem pertaining to the truthfulness of our categorical schemata was solved by Kant by means of the following idea. If our primary media and logical framework of cognition were a mere chimera, a figment of our vivid imagination with no relation to an objective order, then reality would remain an insoluble enigma, an inaccessible realm where no mind may dare to probe and explore. Since the whole cognitive gesture is dependent upon the categorical approach, its legitimacy is *eo ipso* ascertained. The same method is applicable to historical categories. Abraham is the prime historical idea, the basic category that introduces purposefulness and destiny-filled tenseness in our historical experience. Without it, we would forfeit the reasonableness or meta-rationality with which it is endowed.

We experience our historical occurrence in a very peculiar manner. Historical time, in contrast to physical time, is not a mere form enveloping the cosmic process, but rather the historical event itself. It is inseparable from the happening, from the very acting and realizing. What occurs is a time event; what addresses itself to us is a time personality; what emerges is a living time. Hence, to experience a historical figure one must feel the heartbeat of time.

The Jewish historical community has a strange time awareness, one that is often baffling to strangers. Let me illustrate this with an episode that occurred during the Second World War. I received a letter from a Jewish physician in New York in which he enclosed a clipping from an Anglo-Jewish journal published somewhere in Great Britain. The physician, a good friend of mine, implored me in his letter to read the enclosed article and prepare an answer to the writer's attack on traditional Judaism. The author of the article related his experience in a camp in Great Britain where friendly aliens were interned. Among the internees there was a group of young yeshiva students, observant and devout. They paid attention not to current events but to old problems and occurrences that had transpired approximately nineteen hundred years before. They were engaged in an almost interminable discussion about Rabbi Yohanan ben Zakkai's politics on behalf of Yavneh and its scholars. Partisan factions formed in the camp. Some approved of his wise policy of moderation; others disagreed and associated themselves with Rabbi Akiba's policy of political extremism, maintaining that Rabbi Yohanan had blundered by tacitly giving away Jerusalem.

The author of the article listened, pondered the themes that were discussed and that had aroused so much excitement, and asked a very pertinent question. How could young men whose very lives depended upon the outcome of the war live in a remote past and occupy themselves with worthless discussions about archaic events that had no relevance whatsoever as far as their present was concerned, at the same time that they were witnessing world-shaking events such as the invasion of North

Africa by Allied troops and the conference of the Big Two in Casablanca to map out future plans for the war?

The conclusion he arrived at was obviously and unequivocally reminiscent of Toynbee's interpretation of Jewish history, wherein the living Jewish historical drama came to a stop with the rise of Christianity, when our people forfeited its political independence. There is no longer a growing, developing, destiny-conscious Jewish nation, but only a fossilized or mummified community that lives on in memories and thinks in retrospective terms. Using an almost vulgar pseudo-scientific idiom, the author of the article spoke of the frozen stream of the collective consciousness and the absence of continuity and creativity within it. I do not know whether he is still alive or has passed into eternity. But if he is still around, I would like to interview him about that article. Perhaps he has by now changed his opinion about the petrifaction of our historical process. Perhaps we are not as rigid and antiquated as we appear to be. The establishment of the State of Israel would certainly cast a different light upon the whole problem. Our fixity does not, perhaps, eliminate progress or ascent.

It appears to me that the answer to this question is simple enough, and it is to be found in the unique time awareness of our historic community. Our time experience is three-dimensional; past and future address themselves to us in the fleeting moment of the present. We live, of course, in the so-called present, but it can envelop us only if it is interlocked with the other two dimensions. The retrospective mood is one of the major motifs of our time apprehension, and so is the glance that we cast at the silent morrow, at the "not yet," at the expected and fervently desired or hated. Retrospection, in the sense of reliving and reincarnating, and anticipation, which gives rise to a new world, constitute the central motifs of our unique time experience. We see the distances separating the ages and millennia as not so pronounced as in general history.

Modern man has learned how to conquer relatively long stretches of space and geometric distance. Ancient man did not possess this skill. Yet man today has lost completely his memory and time awareness. He has shortened the distances in space but extended the lanes in the time continuum. He is not capable of this miraculous recessional into the centuries and of the bold and grand procession into unactualized and unlived time. He is isolated in the infinitesimal fraction of the now which is, in most cases, disconnected from the before and the after. Both realms are deserted by the pragmatic, utilitarian, *hedone*-seeking man of today, and they form a vast wasteland. Man wanders in the present, not daring to approach the gates of these mysterious kingdoms. He lacks continuity with both his progenitors and his descendants. Man forfeits his historical memory and his great vision, and in losing these two endowments he gives away his capacity for love and devotion, his normative awareness and his idealistic strivings. In the present, usefulness and pleasure reign supreme.

If you should ask me to name the halakhic category that expresses this peculiar time-experience, I would point at the concept of *masorah* or *kabbalah*. These two words designate something unique that cannot be equated with the popular word "tradition." *Masorah* signifies not only formal transmission of knowledge, mores, laws, and a way of life. It implies an awareness of the togetherness of centuries and millennia, of the unity of time within one experience. The *masorah* community is not limited to an aggregate of contemporaries. It is all-inclusive, encompassing past and future, generations that departed life thousands of years ago and those that have not yet been born. It is a community within which the past does not fade away but rather moves into the present, blending with the immediate and direct. In this community, personalities communicate throughout the ages; minds that are thousands of years apart address themselves to each other; heartbeats merge into the historic sound. There is not only transmission of knowledge but also a pouring out of the soul and reincarnation of the master in the person of the disciple.

A Book of Symbols

In his prologue to the Book of Exodus—in some volumes printed as the epilogue to Genesis—Nahmanides (Ramban) writes,

> Scripture has concluded the Book of Genesis, which is *Sefer ha-Yetzirah*, the Book of Creation, pertaining to the emergence of the world and also the emergence of every creature . . . and the happenings or experiences of the patriarchs, which are *ke-inyan yetzirah le-zar'am*, like an act of creation regarding their progeny, as all their experiences are symbols or paradigms—patterns which allude to and anticipate whatever the future holds in store for them. And after Scripture finished the story of creation, it began another book pertaining to the implementation of those allusions and those symbols.

The translation of the symbol into reality, into historical fact, is the Book of Exodus. According to Nahmanides, Exodus tells the same story as Genesis. The latter tells it in symbols; the actors in the drama are three individuals on the stage of history. In Exodus, the actors are a group rather than the three individuals.

Genesis, therefore, should be interpreted on two levels. First of all, it is the story of three concrete individuals and their children, their happy and sad experiences. However, Genesis is not only the story of three individuals; it is also the history of a great people. The three individuals personify the destiny of the people. Abraham is not only the biological father of the people; he is also its spiritual father. He paves the way for our people. His life is a paradigm and a symbol of the future. We speak about *Avraham ha-perati*, the individual Abraham. But at the same time he is also what the homiletical sages later called

Avraham ha-kelali, the universal Abraham. He predicted the historical march toward eternity of the covenantal community chosen by God.

Hazal already were aware of the strange parallelism between the lives of the patriarchs and the historical drama of our people. As the Midrash says, *"Kol mah she-ira [le-Avraham] ira le-vanav*, Whatever happened to [Abraham] happened to his children" (*Midrash Tanhuma, Lekh Lekha* 9, paraphrased by Nahmanides, Gen. 12:6). Similarly, *"Tzei u-khevosh et ha-derekh lifnei vanekha,* Go and pave the way before your children" (Gen. Rabbah 40:6, quoted by Nahmanides, Gen. 12:10). Yet no commentator before Nahmanides exploited these statements as he did. Nahmanides organized them into a philosophy of history: Jewish history is basically the history of the patriarchs. In other words, the lives of the patriarchs contain a blueprint of the Jewish historical process. Nahmanides was not satisfied with a theory of historical paradigms or allusions; he was the father of the idea that Jewish history was predetermined by the activities of the patriarchs.

The question that arises from this is a simple one. By introducing an *a priori* symbolic etiology into Jewish history, Nahmanides seems to have abandoned historical freedom and replaced it with rigid determinism. Every event in Jewish history has been unalterably fixed by paradigmatic action on the part of our ancestors. They acted out *a priori* the major events in our history and laid down rules projecting the patterns of its historical dynamics. Once the divine decree has been translated into metaphorical action, it cannot be changed. The whole of Jewish history turns into a mechanical affair over which human beings have no control. The just ones could not have influenced the course of events that pulled the nation toward the brink of catastrophe, and contrarily, the wicked were unable to accelerate or increase the horrors of *hurban*, destruction. Everything was already acted out and unalterably decided upon. Our ancestors long ago lived these events as historical realities.

What historical role, then, was assigned to the Children of Israel throughout the generations? Were they no longer free to shape their own destiny, to determine their own history? Was acting like marionettes all that was left to them, unable to control their own acts and driven involuntarily to historical doom, *hurban* and exile? The prophets exhorted the people, preached to them, and urged them to mend their ways to placate God's wrath and be saved from destruction and catastrophe. The people were apparently free to invite distress and tragedy or, vice versa, to triumph and live under the Almighty's protection. Judged from the standpoint of Nahmanidean determinism, the Jew could never have escaped the bitter experiences of disaster and *hurban*, since these tragic events were symbolically produced on the historical stage at the time of our patriarchs and thus were predestined as inevitable.

In my opinion, the answer to this question is simple. Certainly, the experiences of the patriarchs foreshadowed the tragic as well as the redeeming events of posterity. Whatever happened to our forefathers was bound to transpire in the life of the nation. The patriarchs indeed spoke the language of premonitory and anticipatory signs. However, the events narrated by the Bible serve as signs or symbols of future events. Any sign or symbol is subject to interpretation, for the semantics of signs and of symbolic language is multiple. Signs can be interpreted in many ways. There is, of course, a message in every biblical scene and event, and this message is related to future scenes and events. Yet the freedom of the people of the Bible has not been curtailed, because a message, like a sign, is subject to interpretation—and the latter is a many-faceted, heterogeneous affair.

We Jews have been taught that the eternal truth of the Torah reveals itself to man by way of many interpretations, and, of course, all of them are true. Halakhic logic, unlike classical logic, is an n-valued logic. The truth, we believe, can be projected against many backgrounds. It may be seen within x number of perspectives, some of which are mutually exclusive. Did not the Gemara say of the two most contradictory systems in the annals of Halakhah, Bet Shammai and Bet Hillel, that *"elu va-elu divrei Elokim hayyim*, both are the words of the living God" (*Eruvin* 13b)? This poly-semantic approach to the Torah is valid, too, with regard to creative historical interpretation. Each event was predetermined by the symbolic acts of the patriarchs. Yet in every generation, how to interpret the event is up to the individual or to the people as a whole. The Jew is free to choose from the many alternative interpretations of the event. The idea that God wills to be realized through the event is the same; yet nonetheless it may be like a beam of white light which, when refracted and dispersed, displays a multitude of colors. The selection of the color is never interfered with by predestination.

Abraham's Sacrifice

Let us take a single example. One of the many events in Abraham's life that are of central significance because of their paradigmatic role in our historical drama is the *Akedah*, the binding of Isaac. According to Nahmanidean historical semantics, the *Akedah* foreshadowed Jewish martyrdom down through the ages. The *Akedah* was the portent of the many sad and tragic situations in which Jews were summoned to bring the supreme sacrifice, their very existence. But the portent was subject to multiple interpretations, and Jews enjoyed the freedom to interpret the strange scene of the *Akedah* in a variety of ways.

The basic idea of the *Akedah* is nurtured by the service awareness. Man is a servant of God. He belongs completely to God—body and soul. God owns human existence at every level, physical, spiritual, and social. Every movement of our muscles is related to God. Every thought that flashes through our minds belongs to Him. Every feeling, every stirring of the soul, every joyful anticipation or sad expectation is not the property of man.

God is the Lord of the world and the master of man. Hence, God from time to time calls upon man to return to Him whatever is His. He demands that man give not a part but the whole of himself. He requires of man to return divine property to its rightful owner. The supreme sacrifice is never too much, since God owns everything and man possesses nothing. "The soul is Yours, and the body is Your handiwork" (High Holy Day prayers). Total sacrifice was decreed by God when He summoned Abraham to offer Isaac on Mount Moriah.

Of course, the idea of sacrifice is a cornerstone of Judaism, and the *Akedah* has inevitably introduced sacrificial action as a part of our historical drama. Yet, as we have said, the drama of the *Akedah* is multi-semantic, lending itself to many interpretations. God demands that man bring the supreme sacrifice, but the fashion in which the challenge is met is for man to determine.

There are two ways in which the total sacrifice is implemented—the physical and the experiential. The choice of the method is up to man. The need for sacrifice was established as an iron law in Jewish history. However, whether man should sacrifice on a physical altar atop some mountain the way God summoned Abraham to do or in the recesses of his personality is man's privilege to determine. Whether the sacrifice consists in physical agony, pain, and extinction of life or in spiritual surrender, humility, and resignation is man's affair. God wills man to choose the altar and the sacrifice.

Abraham implemented the sacrifice of Isaac not on Mount Moriah but in the depths of his heart. He gave up Isaac the very instant God addressed Himself to him and asked him to return his most precious possession to its legitimate master and owner. Immediately, with no arguing or pleading, Abraham surrendered Isaac. He gave him up as soon as the command "and offer him there for a burnt offering" (Gen. 22:2) was issued. Inwardly, the sacrificial act was consummated at once. Isaac no longer belonged to Abraham. Isaac was dead as far as Abraham was concerned. Abraham at that moment experienced the horror, desolation, and black despair of the childless father who has no one to whom he can entrust his most cherished treasure, his vision and hope, and who knows that everything for which he has worked will die with him. Nevertheless, he did not argue. Satan laughed at him. Eliezer and Ishmael had contempt for the old man who had become entangled in an adventure with an invisible God who scoffed at him. Yet Abraham asked no questions. He did not point out the contradiction between God's promise to be with him and his children and the paradoxical command to kill Isaac and burn his flesh.

He proceeded to Mount Moriah. When he arrived there, the sacrifice was a *fait accompli*. In Abraham's mind there was no Isaac, no beloved son, no heir to his spiritual fortune. Abraham came alone, forsaken and forgotten. Isaac's flesh was already consumed by the fires on the altar and had gone up in a pillar of smoke to heaven. There was no need for the physical sacrifice, since experientially Abraham had fulfilled the command before he reached Mount Moriah. All God asked of Abraham was a substitute sacrifice, "and he offered him up for a burnt offering in place of his son" (Gen. 22:13). Had Abraham engaged the Creator in a debate, had he not immediately surrendered Isaac, had he not experienced the *Akedah* in its full awesomeness and frightening helplessness, God would not have sent the angel to stop Abraham from implementing the command. Abraham would have lost Isaac physically.

A Table of Moral Values

The Book of Genesis provides us with a table of moral values. Judaism encourages man to study, to understand, to discover new scientific horizons, to control nature and advance scientifically. However, all that is important only so long as man knows that God reigns behind the beautiful heavens, so long as man is humble and ready to accept the divine norms, so long as man finds in the cosmos not only majesty and grandeur but *kedushah*, sanctity.

There are two sets of norms. One is related to the view that man is a powerful being. Of course, man's specific charisma—the image of God granted at creation—is the source of human might. Man's intellect, if developed and trained properly, is the source of human scientific and technological capabilities which succeed in subjugating some areas of organic and inorganic matter. Truly, one must be very wise to land people on the moon or to send an unmanned vehicle to another planet and get photos of the surface across millions of miles. In a word, man is eager to realize God's command to "fill the world and subjugate it" (Gen. 1:28). If human uniqueness as a power-oriented and power-centered being is the premise upon which our morality is based, then our table of virtues will consist of power categories. If the general norm is power, then the foremost virtue is truth. Sir Francis Bacon realized that those who are not truthful cannot attain power when he coined the phrase "Knowledge is power" (*Religious Meditations, Of Heresies*). Scientific thinking is strict, precise, truthful thinking corroborated by facts. Any deviation from truth renders the thinking valueless and nonsensical.

Next to truth comes courage. To be objective, to not be influenced by prejudice or folk tales and other sentiments, to be cruel in stating facts as they are—these are all indispensable for the concentration of power. In his book *Tycho Brahes Weg zu Gott* ("The Redemption of Tycho Brahe"), Max Brod portrays Tycho Brahe and Johannes Kepler, two astronomers of the sixteenth and seventeenth centuries. Kepler revolutionized astronomy by formulating the famous laws of the orbital movement of the planets—an achievement on the same order as what Newton accomplished in the field of physics. Brod depicts Tycho Brahe as endowed with enormous talent, a genius whose intellectual ability was not inferior to Kepler's. Why, then, was Brahe's contribution so meager and Kepler's so big? It was because Brahe was a sentimentalist with a soft and tender heart. He could not even deny the relevance of astrology. He lacked the intellectual courage to blaze a new path, to think in new categories, to state new laws. He could not break with the past. He failed. Kepler won because he was disciplined and courageous. He did not worship the past, and he disregarded human emotional attachments and commitments. Whatever was scientifically wrong, he denounced. In a word, courage is a *conditio sine qua non* for success.

Powerful man's table of moral values will also include dignity, beauty, and justice in interhuman relations. The latter is the correlate of truth. Whatever truth represents vis-à-vis man as an explorer in his relation to nature, justice represents vis-à-vis one's fellow man in interhuman relations. The common element in both is complete disregard for one's emotional motives. In both, man is insensitive, objective, and completely detached. He is interested in the law, be it the social law of justice or be it the law of nature.

Another morality is centered about pain and suffering. Man is a being who is exposed to pain—to be more precise, to suffering. He is weak and not powerful; if left alone, he is helpless and unhappy. (Let us not be perturbed by the dialectical morality related to two contradictory portrayals of man, since both are true. He is powerful as well as weak.) This passional morality has a separate set of values that includes sympathy, charity, and friendship. All of them revolve around *hesed*, loving-kindness. While the first set of values is concerned with the independence of the intellect, with the free mind that rejects any intervention of human emotion no matter how noble, the second set requires us to act at times in accordance with our hearts, to let constructive, cathartic emotions guide our intellect or will in the making of decisions. Judaism does not reject the morality of detachment and strictly objective activity. It has always been aware of the significance of man's intellectual uniqueness and scientific thinking. However, it accepts, in addition to the morality of power, a morality of suffering that demands involvement rather than detachment, not a person-object relationship but a person-person one. While the morality of power speaks of man as an observer or onlooker who is interested in finding the truth, the morality of involvement revolves about man-sufferer and man-redeemer who is concerned with the destiny of others.

In fact, there are two sets of divine attributes as well. One set deals with God's omnipotence and majesty. Another set is concerned with God's boundless *hesed*—or, to be more exact, His total involvement. The human being is commanded to follow in God's footsteps with regard to both the category of might and the categories of humility and unlimited kindness. The famous adage of R. Yohanan, "Wherever you find [mentioned in the Scriptures] the power of the Holy One, blessed be He, you also find [mentioned] His humility" (*Megillah* 31a), emphasizes the dialectical character of the attributes that represent the table of the basic norms. Consequently, we are commanded to comply with a dialectical ethic, one of *gevurah* and the other of *hesed*.

These norms are sometimes mutually exclusive. When we must act in a situation in which there is conflict between these two norms, we have to be guided by the Halakhah. At times we are told to act in accordance with *hesed* and at other times with *gevurah*. Let me give an example. Should the sinner be punished, or should the court look for mitigating circumstances and accept his penitential commitments? Should we have justice or mercy, complete detachment or involvement? Our sages said, "*Ve-rav hesed, matteh kelappei hesed*" (*Rosh ha-Shanah* 17a): preference is given to *hesed*. Otherwise God would not befriend the *ba'al teshuvah*. In fact, the Yerushalmi says that we inquired of wisdom and of prophecy, and they both agreed that the sinner should be punished; the Almighty, however, disagreed with them and said, "Let him repent and he will be forgiven" (*Makkot* 2:4, fol. 31d). *Hesed* prevailed and overruled truth.

However, at times man must not forgive evil but must fight it and try to eradicate it. In particular, organized evil must be wiped off the face of the earth. As an example, consider the commandment of destroying Amalek. Amalek represents not a race but a group that is committed to an immoral life, holding that deeds that increase human misery are moral. The Nazi movement was and still is identical with Amalek. In dealing with people so monstrous, *gevurah* overrides *hesed*.

Abraham personified both the ethic of victory and justice and the ethic of mercy and involvement. Abraham pursued the four kings, smote them, and pursued them unto Hobah. He practiced stern justice—no consideration, no pardon, no mercy. Victory was the watchword, for negotiating with politicians who are out to destroy is suicidal. Yet he pleaded with the Almighty to forgive Sodom. He felt that the situation in Sodom was not hopeless. Ten great teachers and leaders might save the city. Abraham's great moral gesture was related not to strength but to kindness, to the involvement of the I in the distress of the thou. Abraham announced the morality of suffering.

Abraham's table of moral virtues commenced with *hakhnasat orehim*, hospitality. To be hospitable to newcomers or strangers was his first and foremost norm. This virtue is emphasized time and again as Abraham's characteristic trait. It was most dramatically expressed when the three angels came to visit him after his circumcision while he sat "at the entrance of his tent in the heat of the day" (Gen. 18:1). The Talmud tells us that the Almighty increased the heat of the day so that Abraham would not be troubled by travelers (*Bava Metzi'a* 86b). But when the Almighty perceived that Abraham was saddened because no travelers came by, He brought three angels in the form of men. Abraham felt unhappy when he could not entertain wanderers.

Although God had come to visit him, Abraham excused himself when he noticed the three travelers and asked the Almighty to wait for him while he attended to his guests. Practicing hospitality to man is a more important mitzvah than receiving the

Almighty (*Shabbat* 127a). Hospitality is not just *a* virtue; it is *the* virtue, the greatest and most sublime one.

Lot deserted Abraham; he betrayed him and settled in Sodom. But Lot practiced hospitality even while he forsook other Abrahamic practices. He contemptuously cast away many of Abraham's principles and practices, but he could not help but be hospitable. His sojourn in Sodom, no matter how corrupting, could not uproot the virtue of *hakhnasat orehim*. Almost mechanically he said, "Behold now, my lords, turn in, I beseech you, to your servant's house, and remain all night, and wash your feet, and you shall rise up early, and go on your way" (Gen. 19:2). Abraham's vocabulary! Abraham's mannerism! Abraham's persistence! He could not forget these. The guests refused at the beginning because they wanted to test him. Is there still a spark of the holy flame that Abraham ignited? He passed the test. "He pressed them very much" (Gen. 19:3).

Studying the Bible

When we study the Bible, we must be concerned about two things. We must understand the semantics of the word, and we must understand the spiritual message of the Bible. There is an enormous literature of biblical criticism, and the problem with that literature is that it completely misses the spiritual message. It introduces modern literary forms and criteria which are completely inapplicable to the Bible. It does not understand that the Bible is not a book of stories but a book of a great spiritual message and way of life—a new code. Wherever they see contradictions, I see harmony. And wherever they see conflict between two views, I see uniformity.

Besides our understanding of the semantics of the words, their style, and the historical background, there is a great spiritual message, a *kerygma*. The Torah is not concerned exclusively with past events; it is also concerned with our thoughts, our feelings, and our commitments. The Torah relates not only to *hovot ha-evarim*, "the duties of the limbs," but also what R. Bahya ibn Pakuda calls *hovot ha-levavot*, "duties of the heart," duties of the spirit, duties related to one's emotional life—when to rejoice, when not to rejoice, when to mourn, when not to mourn, when to defy and when to surrender. A Torah life embraces not only our external deeds but also our inner world.

In my opinion, that is what R. Simai meant when he said, "There is no *parashah* that does not contain [an allusion to] the resurrection of the dead" (*Yalkut Shim'oni*, *Ha'azinu*, 942; also *Midrash Tanna'im*, Deut. 32:2). In every *parashah* in the Torah, we can discover an article of faith, an *ikkar ha-Yahadut*, implicitly contained in it. If we examine the text closely, we may find a treasure hidden in one word or one letter. This is certainly true of the first book of the Bible. Human destiny is reflected in Genesis—human triumph and defeat, human greatness and smallness, the potential of what man is capable of achieving, his opportunities and even his defiance of the Master of the Universe.

When we speak about Abraham, we must always remember that the Bible is not only a book narrating events that transpired so many millennia ago. It speaks of events that are still taking place before our eyes. Actually, it is a book not only of Abraham but also of the destiny of our people. We are an eternal people, and our destiny is eternal—and the *Humash* is the book of our destiny. That is the Nahmanidean concept of *ma'aseh avot siman la-banim*.

❧ From Adam to Abraham: The Fall and Rise of Monotheism

The Descent into Idolatry

The story of Abraham's early years—how he found God—is not recorded in the Bible. His biography is very fragmentary; only certain episodes of his life are singled out. Abraham is the one who recognized God and proclaimed to the world a new doctrine, a new moral code. We would have liked the *Humash* to tell us about his sleepless nights when he was struggling with himself, when he began to rebel against pagan society, when he left that society. But we know nothing about him until his mature age. The Midrash fills in some of the blanks, and Maimonides made use of these to compile a biography of Abraham, to project his image, his profile.

Maimonides' primary purpose in including a biography of Abraham in the opening chapter of *Hilkhot Avodat Kokhavim* was to embed Abraham within his disquisition on the nature of religion and idolatry. He therefore prefaces his description of the birth and early years of Abraham with a historico-philosophic discourse.

History of religion looks upon monotheism as the result of a long evolutionary process, as the faith of a civilized society that has succeeded in freeing man from his environment. Religion, so say the historians, has grown with man. It is one of the aspects of man's emergent evolution from the cave to the laboratory, from the noise of the jungle to the music of Mozart and Beethoven.

Primitive man, history of religion asserts, believed in spirits residing in trees, in gods abiding in the golden bough or in ferocious beasts. Gradually, along with his liberation from the jungle and the cave, man freed himself from what he had once considered the invincible horrors of the forest and began to worship more abstract deities, representing or symbolizing ideas or universal phenomena such as power, beauty, and love. Gradually, with the discovery that the universe is not a multiple but a unified affair regulated by natural laws rooted in a single principle, man found the one God.

In other words, the cultic gesture of mankind was of a very primitive nature. Only after a long, progressive march and a piecemeal ascent to the great heights of a civilized orientation did it find monotheism. The latter lies not at the root, but at the apex of man's cultic life. Civilized religion, like universal civilization, is a product of human cultural evolution.

Maimonides, however, has a different and original approach to human cultic life. Man started out with monotheism, the highest form of worship, he says. Later, however, man fell into gross error and began to serve idols or spirits. According to anthropology, idolatry is the cult of aboriginal primitive man, and religion, as an expression of humankind's civilizing consciousness and civilizing gesture, keeps pace with the emergence of general civilization. For Maimonides, faith in God is not a cultural accomplishment to which only civilized man is entitled. Faith is a redeeming act without which man's whole existence turns into a meaningless, absurd phenomenon. Man without faith is an illegitimate being, damned to nihility; he lacks a *raison d'être*. Faith spells salvation. Everyone is entitled to salvation, and everyone must be redeemed. Primitive man and progressive man, simpleton and philosopher, ignorant man and scientist alike—all of them need faith. Hence, faith is a non-cultural apocalyptic experience which is attainable at all levels of human evolution. God calls man to His service not only from within civilized society but also from the jungle and the forest, from the halls of wisdom as well as from the herd of frightened primitives. God does not require that man be scientifically versed or technologically developed in order to disclose to him the mystery of faith. In general, what are we in relation to the omnipotent, omniscient, eternal, and infinite Creator, if not ridiculous, nonsensical, ignorant, and foolish beings? So what difference does it make whether or not we are members of what we call a civilized society? After all, "the preeminence of man"— even civilized man—"over the beast is naught, for all is vanity" (Eccl. 3:19).

Hence, says Maimonides, man, who was created in the image of God, has known God since his appearance on the face of the globe. Aboriginal man, first man, knew only one God. In his simplicity and naiveté he did not worship finite creatures. He knew the truth.

Maimonides describes the development of paganism and the organization of pagan priesthoods, and so forth. Paganism encroached upon everyone. "As time passed, the honored and revered name of God, *ha-shem ha-nikhbad ve-ha-nora,* was forgotten by mankind and vanished from their lips and minds, and they were unable even to recognize Him" (*Hilkhot Avodat Kokhavim* 1:2). Maimonides here uses two attributes, two epithets, *ha-nikhbad ve-ha-nora.* We can find a clue to the Maimonidean semantics of these two words by finding a parallel passage where the term is explained by its context:

> It is incumbent upon us to love and fear God *ha-nikhbad ve-ha-nora*, as it is written, "You shall love the Lord your

God with all your heart and all your soul" (Deut. 6:5) and it is written, "The Lord your God you shall fear" (Deut. 6:13). And what is the way that will lead to the love of Him and the fear of Him? When a person contemplates His great and wondrous works and creatures and from them obtains a glimpse of His wisdom, which is incomparable and infinite, he will straightway love Him, praise Him, glorify Him, and long with an exceeding longing to know His great Name, even as David said, "My soul thirsts for the Lord, for the living God" (Ps. 42:3). (*Hilkhot Yesodei ha-Torah* 2:1–2)

Man must concentrate upon creation and explore it. Maimonides does not speak of the objective, cold knowledge of the scientist in the laboratory. He speaks of a passionate knowledge which man experiences. (Let me say about myself that I experience the Gemara I am learning and teaching. When I study Abaye and Rava, it is a drama for me, not a question of classification of concepts and definitions. If people say that I am a good teacher, it is not because of my knowledge, but due to my experiential approach to the Gemara. The Gemara becomes a part of me.) The strong desire to understand is intoxicating; man becomes an addict of knowledge—a wonderful experience! Man is overcome by a great passion to be in communion with the Almighty and as close to Him as possible. He wants to sing and extol and to praise and glorify the name of the Almighty. There is a romance between man and God. Man has an uncontrollable, powerful longing, an invisible craving and desire to unite with God, to be close to Him, to submerge in Him.

God is fascinating to man. The relationship between man and God is a magnetic one. God pulls man toward Himself like a giant magnet. The humanity of man consists in that pull, in that invincible force which drags him toward God, "My soul thirsts for the Lord, for the living God" (Ps. 42:3). One satisfies thirst by drinking water. God Himself is metaphorically portrayed as a wellspring. "They have forsaken Me, a spring of living water, to hew cisterns, broken cisterns, that will hold no water" (Jer. 2:13). Crystal-clear water keeps on flowing, and man is thirsty. This is love for God Who fascinates and attracts people, Who pulls them toward Himself. "*Nikhbadot,* glorious things, are spoken of You" (Ps. 87:3). If you love a person very much, you try to get close to him. There is an additional response to the emotion of love: to praise, to sing, to write prose, to compose hymns. *Ha-E-l ha-nikhbad* means *E-l mehullal ba-tishbahot.* When we say *Pesukei de-Zimrah,* when we sing a hymn to God, when we say *Hallel,* we express this ecstatic love.

Maimonides continues in the same passage:

> And when he ponders these matters, he will recoil frightened, and realize that he is a small creature, lowly and obscure, endowed with slight and slender intelligence, standing in the presence of Him who is perfect in knowledge. And so David said, "When I consider Your heavens, the work of Your fingers—what is man that You are mindful of him?" (Ps. 8:4–5).

Nora is the opposite of *nikhbad.* Man is engaged in a forward movement toward God, and he wants to come as close to God as possible. But at the very moment that he feels he is very close to God, fear arises and expresses itself in a movement of recoil. Love is a surging forward; fear means retreat and withdrawal. Man is frightened, for how can a finite being be embraced by Infinity and at the same time retain its identity? *Ha-nora* means that one cannot come too close to Him.

The real God experience, according to Maimonides, expresses itself in a very strange dialectical movement. First, the desire is a mad passion, an ecstatic love that is beautifully portrayed in the Song of Songs. We see there, however, that the lovers never meet. He is in love with her, and she is in love with him; why don't they meet? After all, she wandered about during the day and asked the caretakers of the vineyards and the shepherds if they had seen him. She came home at night disappointed, disillusioned, and went to sleep. Suddenly, there is a knock on the door. The beloved has come. She has a debate with herself, to open the door or not to open. In the meantime, her beloved leaves, and then she decides to open the door. But when she opens the door, he is gone. This is the dialectical movement! The *dod*, the lover, is the Holy One, and the *ra'ayah,* the beautiful shepherdess, is *Keneset Yisrael*. There is a search for God; there is a tremendous drive to come as close to Him as possible. She is intoxicated with love; she is an addict of love, she is in a state of ecstasy. When the *dod* finally knocks on her door, she is frightened, because she is afraid that once she meets the *dod* she will disappear. The *dod* is infinity, and she is just a finite being.

This is exactly what Maimonides described with the phrase *ha-nikhbad ve-ha-nora*. According to Maimonides (in the second part of the *Guide),* behind the cosmic dynamics there is the interplay of two forces, attraction and daunting, fascination and repulsion. Through these two forces, God makes the cosmos tick and be alive. Maimonides believes that "this Universe, in its entirety, is nothing else but one individual being" (*Guide* I:72), and what is true of the cosmos is true of the individual person as well. The spiritual life of human beings, like the cosmos, is the result of this dialectical movement, coming close and retreating. It means to fly toward God and fly away from Him, forward and backward. When idolatry arose, this awareness "vanished from the lips of everyone." They forgot the basic principle that is responsible for existence: love of God and fear of God, moving forward and backward, advancing and retreating.

A Triple Commitment

Maimonides enumerates a triple estrangement from God: God's name vanished from man's lips, God disappeared from his awareness, and man forfeited his ability to recognize God. From this we may deduce that a commitment to God expresses itself in three ways: God's name is on one's lips, one possesses an awareness of God's presence, and one has the ability to identify or recognize God. There must be a threefold commitment: speech, mind, and spontaneous intuition.

The fundamental commandment of Judaism is not to simply know God but to be aware of Him. We may compare human awareness of God with a mother's awareness of her child. It is constant, not intermittent. She cannot forget the child or see herself without seeing her child. In the same manner, one must always be aware of God's presence—not only that there is a God, but that He is near. God is, on the one hand, ineffable, inexpressible, incomprehensible, distant, and far; on the other hand, He is very, very close. This awareness must be a permanent state of mind, not a transient mood, dependent upon environmental facts, that can be aroused by applying extraneous, mundane stimuli such as music, magnificent architectural masterpieces, spiraling cathedrals, or the soft solemn sound of an organ. Awareness of God is more primordial, more aboriginal; it is a steady state of mind, not just a fleeting, capricious mood. But Judaism is very practical and realistic; it insists that any inner experience be translated into halakhic terms, into practical behavioral categories.

The steady, acute awareness of God's presence cleanses man of vulgarity, coarseness, shamelessness, and indecent behavior. Even a legitimate act can be performed in a saintly manner or in a coarse, vulgar, and shameless manner. Nahmanides (Lev. 19:2) speaks about the quality of saintliness in one's life: "One can lead a vulgar life and still live in accordance with the Law." However, awareness of the presence of God leads man to a saintly, moral life.

To know and understand God means to follow in His footsteps, to imitate Him—what the medieval philosophers call *imitatio Dei*, what Maimonides calls *lehidamot el Hashem* (*Hilkhot De'ot* 1:6). To be sure, there is an element of arrogance in trying to be like God; but apparently there is a special dispensation allowing man to set this goal for himself. The Gemara speaks of "You shall walk after the Lord your God" (Deut. 13:5): "Just as He dressed the naked . . . so should you dress the naked; the Holy One, blessed be He, visited the sick . . . so should you visit the sick; the Holy One, blessed be He, comforted mourners . . . so should you comfort mourners; the Holy One, blessed be He, buried the dead . . . so should you bury the dead" (*Sotah* 14a).

Maimonides said that if not for the moral, practical aspect, we would not be allowed to speak of God's attributes at all (*Guide* I:54). He is beyond us, we cannot comprehend His ways, and therefore we have no right even to express His praise. We are licensed to praise Him because in doing so we also formulate the moral law. Maimonides distinguished between essential attributes and actional attributes. The essential attributes, according to Maimonides, cannot even be pronounced. God is incomprehensible, ineffable, and inexpressible. However, the actional attributes have practical significance. If "The Lord is near to all who call upon Him, to all who call upon Him in truth" (Ps. 145:18), then we, too, should be very close to people and respond to their petitions. It means we should have a sense of compassion and sympathy. An inquiry into God's actional attributes is *eo ipso* an inquiry into the nature of the good and the nature of the law.

But what are the sources of this knowledge? How can we acquire it? Knowledge in general is acquired by perceptions and sensations which are later translated or interpreted by our reason. We know the world because we perceive the world and then our perceptions are translated into ideas. Knowledge is a result of experience. We do not experience God *per se* the way we experience sight and sound, but we can experience His reflected image, so to speak. The mirror that reflects the beautiful face of divinity, His countenance, is the prophets. God reveals Himself through the stupendous, mighty, and boundless cosmos, and also with the gentle word spoken in a whisper to the prophet.

The two experiences complement each other. The prophets interpreted how to utilize the cosmic experience and how the cosmic experience could lead man toward the realization of his moral destiny. To know God means to study the word of God, which was incorporated and crystallized in the Bible.

Thus, *da'at Hashem* is one element of our commitment to God. When Maimonides says that God vanished from the minds of the idolaters, this means that they lost the awareness of His steady presence. This loss of awareness led to their vulgarization, for what ennobles man is the awareness of God. Dismissing God from one's mind leads also to the loss of the moral code, because the moral code is nurtured by our knowledge of God and His ways. In contrast, the acute awareness of God ennobles man, redeems him from vulgarity and opens up to him the moral code.

There is another element in *da'at Hashem,* one that will be important when we pick up the biography of Abraham. To know God also means to have a desire to share one's knowledge with others, to have a longing to teach people, to bring the message to the ignorant and insensitive or to those unfortunate ones who have not had the opportunity to learn and to study. A man who is happy and does not want to teach others is not necessarily cruel and selfish. But he is not a scholar. A real scholar cannot contain what he knows within himself; he explodes. Knowledge entails a dynamic element; the knower becomes restless, the truth cries out from the inner recesses of his personality, and he must tell others.

The second principle of commitment is that the name of God must be on one's lips. "This book of the Torah shall not depart out of your mouth; but you shall meditate therein day and night" (Joshua 1:8). Why is it necessary to not only think of God and be aware of Him, but also to verbalize and externalize this awareness? Judaism has always required that man objectify his thoughts and feelings. The Torah did not underrate the role of subjectivity in religion, but the Torah was suspicious if one tries to reduce religion to subjectivity. *Avodah she-ba-lev*, worship of the heart, is a state of mind. But apparently the Halakhah was not satisfied with having *avodah she-ba-lev* arrested within the human personality. It required of us to externalize it through the recital of a standardized, fixed text of *tefillah*. Emotions come and go; therefore, we must act out our emotions. If we have God in mind, if we are aware of Him, we must pronounce it, verbalize it, say it in words.

I know that when I prepare a *shi'ur*, if I write out everything, and everything is neatly arranged, then when I deliver the *shi'ur*, it does not require so much energy and is not a strain for me. But if I don't write out a *shi'ur*—no matter how well I understand it—and instead I have to work it out during the delivery, it is a tremendous strain. No matter how clearly a person understands something, if he has not written it out, formulated it in words and sentences, it is still amorphous and formless.

The same is true of confession. It is not enough to repent in one's heart; one must formulate his confession to God in words and pronounce it verbally. Why? Man will discover many things he did not understand before when he tries to formulate his thoughts in words. That is why it is necessary for a person who is in love with God to not hide it, but to speak up, to express it, to verbalize it.

Judaism believes that words *per se* are the most powerful weapon God has provided man. Judaism believes in the power of the mind and the majesty of the word. Through the word, God created the world. God did not need words to create the world, but He chose the word as the instrument of creation in order to teach us that we can create the world through the word—and can destroy the world through the word. The word can be the most creative power in man's hands, but it can also be the most destructive power given to man. That is why Judaism is almost merciless with regard to *lashon ha-ra*, evil speech, and why it takes so seriously the issues of perjury, vows, and oaths.

In Judaism, the word is the mark of one's identity as a human being, in contradistinction to a beast or brute. In medieval Hebrew, the name for man is *medabber*, the "speaker." Judaism believes in the potency of the word. It is not just a sound, it is not just phonetics—it has a mystical quality to it. Hence man's awareness of God must be objectified in the word. "And they all open their mouth in holiness and purity, in song and hymn, and bless, praise, glorify, revere, sanctify, and declare the kingship of God" (*Siddur*).

The third principle of commitment to God is *hakkarah*. This term is always related to recognition or identification:

> And he recognized him not (*ve-lo hikkiro*), because his hands were hairy as his brother Esau's hands; so he blessed him (Gen. 27:23).

> Recognize now (*hakker na*) whether it be your son's long-sleeved garment or not; and he recognized it . . . (Gen. 37:32-33).

> Recognize I pray thee (*hakker na*) whose are these, the signet, the strip and the staff? (Gen. 38:25).

When Maimonides says that the idolators "*lo hikiruhu,*" he means to say that they were alienated and estranged from the Almighty to such an extent that when God confronted them or addressed Himself to them they failed to recognize Him. This is the worst alienation, a complete fall away from God.

The faculty of recognition, of establishing identity, is, to a great extent, a puzzling phenomenon. *Hakkarah* in halakhic terms has a double meaning. First, it means identification by indicating certain characteristic or marks on an object. Whoever studied the Talmudic chapter *Elu Metzi'ot* knows that a lost object is returned to the person who claims to be its rightful owner if the latter can describe it by marks or signs. The

Talmud questioned the reliability of identification by marks and queried whether the latter is a biblical or rabbinical institution. Of course, it is a probability problem; the reliability is dependent upon the nature of the mark. Therefore, we have divided marks, or *simanim,* into three classes, the highest is the distinguished or specific mark, *siman muvhak.*

The second halakhic meaning of *hakkarah* is identification of an object from a general impression of its form without stating particular marks. This type of recognition, *tevi'at ayin,* is precipitated by the apprehension of the configuration or of the whole as such.

The Halakhah considers general recognition far superior to identification by guessing marks. Configurative recognition is solid, a certainty. Psychologically, the difference between *hakkarah* by telling marks and by recognizing the whole is as follows. Identification by *simanim* is not instantaneous; it consists in an act of inferring: the object belongs to me because I know the mark that is characteristic of this object. If it were not mine, how would I know about the mark? Of course, there are two possibilities: either I saw the object before, or there are two objects with the identical characteristics. The decision by the court to accept the sign as piece of evidence is based on probability and statistics. However, identification based upon a general impression of the configuration or the whole is spontaneous, instantaneous.

It has been proven by modern psychology and philosophy that recognition is not based upon the act of reasonable inferring or concluding. The logos in general plays no role, or a very limited one. Even animals recognize their masters, and infants recognize their mothers. "The ox knows his owner" (Isa. 1:3). It is an instinctual, spontaneous performance. Of course, with regard to the animal, recognition, like all instinctual drives, is just a mechanical push, a non-conscious reaction. (We don't know exactly what provokes this reaction.) In the case of humans, recognition is an intuitive act. This act of recognition is not in response to a single color, perception, shape, or any other sensation, but rather in response to a countenance, to a face as a whole, as a configuration. The faculty of recognition is activated at times by intangible qualities which one intuits, as opposed to perceiving. Somehow recognition is a result of the mute response of object to subject or of subject to subject. The distinctive perception of sound or color is irrelevant. You may recognize a person by the fleeting wink of an eye.

Recognition of God is an art in itself. It is a double one: by *simanim* and by *tevi'at ayin*. The most exalted recognition is achieved through *tevi'at ayin*. How does one recognize the Almighty? At times we meet Him on the street. He greets first: "Peace, peace, to him that is far off and to him that is near, says the Lord" (Isa. 57:19). Quite often we ignore His greeting; we don't recognize Him.

We know the story about the divine initiation of Samuel as prophet. He was a young child when God addressed Himself to him. In a moving description of the episode, the Bible tells us:

> And the lamp of God was not yet gone out, and Samuel was laid down to sleep in the temple of the Lord, where the ark of God was. Then the Lord called Samuel and he said, "Here am I." And he ran unto Eli and said: "Here am I, for you did call me." And he said, "I called not; lie down again." And the Lord called yet again Samuel, and Samuel arose and went to Eli . . . Now Samuel did not yet know the Lord, neither was the word of the Lord revealed to him. And the Lord called Samuel again the third time, and he arose and went to Eli and said: "Here am I." And Eli perceived that the Lord was calling the child. Therefore Eli said unto Samuel: "Go, lie down; and it shall be if you be called that you shall say, 'Speak, Lord, for your servant hears.' So Samuel went and lay down in his place. And the Lord came, and stood, and called as at the other times, "Samuel, Samuel." Then

Samuel said, "Speak, Lord, for your servant hears" (I Sam. 3:3-10).

This wonderful story conveys to us that the call coming from God is identical to the call coming from man. It possesses the same sounds, the same resonance, the same physical qualities. From the standpoint of perceptional psychology, the Divine call does not differ from the human. However, there is some mysterious quality in the call coming from God. It is very elusive, and at the same time frightening and gladdening, and it cannot be explained in categories of physiological psychology. There is an irresistible pull, an element of overpowering fascination. The call, if ignored at first, continues to come through time and again.

Let me introduce another idea. We know that the acceptance of *nevu'ah*, prophecy, is a tenet in Judaism. The article of prophecy states that God communicates with man and reveals to him His will. We also know that there is *ru'ach ha-kodesh*, divine inspiration. What is the difference between *nevu'ah* and *ru'ach ha-kodesh*? When communicated to the prophet, God's word comes from infinity, from the mysterious transcendence, from the outside, from the beyond. However, God's word at the level of *ru'ach ha-kodesh* comes from within; God addresses Himself to man from the awe-inspiring recesses of the human personality. God reveals Himself to man from *ma'amakim*, the depths of the human consciousness. It is the same word. At both levels, God speaks and man listens. However, in the realm of *nevu'ah* God speaks from the outside, and in the case of *ru'ach ha-kodesh* from within man.

While *nevu'ah* came to a close with Haggai, Zechariah, and Malachi, the holy divine inspiration did not disappear completely. From generation to generation, there are great charismatic individuals whom God blesses with some kind of divine inspiration (such as the Ari, the Vilna Gaon, and the Besht).

I would say that a spark of *ru'ach ha-kodesh* is to be found in the soul of every Jew. God addresses Himself to the Jew, calls him from within, and awaits an answer. Some respond after a while; some ignore Him. How can man determine God's presence or absence from the sanctuary He dedicates in every soul? Is it possible to recognize God's presence? The answer is yes!

The Halakhah has equated *simhah*, the emotion of joy, with *lifnei Hashem*, the awareness of God's presence. On the other hand, grief and sadness are indicative of the metaphysical vacuity caused by God's absence from or abandonment of man. The Halakhah has warned man, has tried to teach the individual to recognize God in every joy-experience, in every beat of a happy heart, in every tremor of fulfillment, in every ray of light that enlightens us and makes life worth living. One should recognize God in every achievement that gladdens the soul, in every day spent meaningfully, and in the fatigue the creative person experiences after having completed his task satisfactorily.

In a word, if man is happy, if he has a song on his lips and a melody in his heart, then let him recognize God. For how can a man rejoice if God has left him, and if everything in him and around him is dreary and bleak?

As a matter of fact, the duty to thank and praise God— *Hallel*, *birkat ha-Gomel*, or the hymnal part of prayer—is based upon our notion that wherever man is successful, satisfied and happy, God is with him. We greet God with *shirot ve-tishbachot*, songs and praises. This is an old tradition. Whenever one can point at the Almighty and say, "This is my God," then he is obligated to sing a hymn. Song is an expression of happiness and joy.

On the other hand, Judaism has taught us also the art of recognizing the absence of God, the ontological vacuum created by His departure. In moments of distress and crisis, when man lives through the dark night of the lonely soul, man should experience the fright and terror of being alone in an empty world.

The dark night of loneliness may be precipitated by disease, death, economic ruin, or social failure. At other times, the dark night encroaches upon man because he inevitably must encounter existential failure and disillusionment. Self-downgrading is an act indicative of human dignity and singularity. Man is a restless being. He must live through frustration and self-ridicule. Every one of us knows those emotions, this kind of anguish. Of course, the very instant man enters the dark night of loneliness, he must recognize that God has absented Himself. At such an hour, man's prayer does not consist of hymns and odes but of petition and intercession. At such an hour, man prays *mi-ma'amakim*, from the depths.

Recognition of God's presence and absence at certain moments leads to a proper interpretation of events both in the lives of individuals and in the life of the community. To read history properly and to interpret it in the light of God's absence or presence is a prime duty of the Jew. This is implied by the Nahmanidean doctrine of *ma'aseh avot siman la-banim*. "Remember the days of old, consider the years of many generations; ask your father, and he will declare unto you, your elders, and they will tell you" (Deut. 32:7).

Man must have an excellent ear in order to hear the footsteps of the Lord who walks in the Garden of Eden or in the garden of human history. Sometimes God walks in the direction of the rising sun, and at other times God walks toward the setting sun. Yet, in either case, we must beware of the danger that, like Adam and Eve, man will purposely try to escape reality and hide upon hearing the footsteps of the Lord. Otherwise, he will descend to the level of Abraham's contemporaries, who could not hear the call, who could not even recognize God.

Abraham's Birth

Paganism encroached upon everyone, scholar and simpleton alike. And, Maimonides says, "The world moved on in this fashion, *holekh u-mitgalgel*, until the pillar of the world, our patriarch Abraham, was born" (*Hilkhot Avodat Kokhavim* 1:2). Actually, "moved on" would have been the right translation if Maimonides had used the word *noheg*. *Noheg* means motion toward a certain destination. But *mitgalgel* means aimless, directionless movement, like an object rolling down a hill carried by the external force of gravity. In other words, *mitgalgel* signifies man's surrender to the elemental, external forces that push him from the outside, when man becomes an object. A person moves because he decides to move. When a person is pushed and rolls down the hill, he acts not like a person but like an object, for the movement is due not to a free decision from within, to an inner quest or a vision or a desired objective, but rather to a blind mechanical push. *Mitgalgel* means unsupervised, non-directed, purposeless, and destinationless motion drifting toward disaster. Greek tragedy portrays such irreversible motion as symbolizing uncontrollable fate. Man surrenders to fate because he has no choice. It is the clash between man as a person and man as an object.

Judaism was unwilling to accept the Greek tragic view. It believed in man and had unlimited faith in him. Man can always, even under the worst of circumstances, act like a persona and not be a *mitgalgel*. The Greeks, despite their enormous culture, had no faith in man. They had faith in man's intellect, but not in his courageous freedom. While Judaism believed in man's intellect, it did not consider the intellect the most important aspect of humanity. It believed in man's freedom, in his capability to plan his own life and not to subject himself to—if I may use the term as a metaphor—the gravitational, mechanical pull. That is the reason any spiritual ascent of man is described as climbing—one defies gravity to climb a hill.

Maimonides says that before Abraham was born, man was not a persona. He was an object who surrendered to the blind, mechanical forces of the environment. Man had lost his freedom and his faith in himself.

Without Abraham, without a great moral teacher, pagan mankind can be divided into two groups: *benei basar* and *rish'ei aretz*, children of flesh and wicked of the earth. We pray in

Aleinu that the *benei basar* will call upon God's name and the *rish'ei aretz* will turn to Him. The Bible tells us stories about both groups in the passages preceding Abraham's birth, because without them we cannot understand Abraham. The generation of the flood consisted of *benei basar,* "for all flesh had corrupted its way upon the earth" (Gen. 6:12). The builders of the Tower of Babel—the generation of the dispersion, of which Nimrod is a symbol—were *rish'ei aretz.*

Judaism hated paganism not only because it is based upon superstition and falsity. Paganism preaches a way of life, not just idolatrous cultic services. Paganism actually preaches two systems of morality. One system is based upon over-sensitivity to unredeemed carnal beauty. The generation of the flood was permissive, surrendering to beauty, carnal pleasure, comfort, and convenience. "The distinguished men saw that the daughters of men were fair, and they took for themselves wives of all whom they chose" (Gen. 6:2). The pagan way of life rests upon the idea of egocentric hedonism. Free man is expected to reject any restrictive norm interfering with his hedonic freedom. The permissive society is a pagan society heading toward disaster. The permissive society consists of *benei basar*, children of the flesh who are obedient to the flesh and its biological pressures. The main sin of this pagan society consists in its exploiting nature for the sake of human enjoyment without people accepting responsibility for the very acts they enjoy. In a word, hedonic society, the generation of the flood, drove itself and the environment to annihilation. Modern man is very mighty; he is a wizard as far as intellectual achievement is concerned, mighty *benei elohim.* The same man who split the atom is tempted by vulgar beauty; he surrenders to enjoyment, to carnal pleasure, which is vulgar and coarse in itself. This is one way of life, and this is what happened during the ten generations from Adam to Noah. They were *mitgalgel* until they reached the bottom.

However, there is another way of life, one that does not consist in a permissive society, but is unconditionally dedicated to a certain idea or doctrine, a certain philosophy or a particular economic or political system. While man in the hedonic society wants to be free and to let no norm interfere with his enjoyment of his way of life, man in the other society is enslaved by a rigid system. This pagan gives preference to doctrine over living souls, to the figment of some utopian idea over human reality. This society is ruled by power-hungry men who want to possess and own the individual—or rather to deprive the individual of his soul, to depersonalize him and convert him into a machine, into an object. It is out to organize and convert mankind into an army and to introduce uniformity. It does not believe that each individual has his own approach to life and his own unique talents. It tells people how to write, how to paint, how to engage in sculpture, how to think scientifically. It believes in the primacy of machine over man, the primacy of dead matter over the living soul. This approach is represented by the generation of the dispersion, who defied the Almighty and sought to build "a tower with its top in the heavens" (Gen. 11:4). They rejected the transcendental norm and substituted their own law for the transcendental law. The builders of the Tower of Babel depersonalized man so thoroughly that they would ignore a man who fell off the building, but would cry when a stone or a brick fell (*Pirkei de-Rabbi Eliezer* 24).

If the moral norm is rejected, man becomes a member of either a hedonic society or a society which believes that its norm is superior. "The world moved on in this fashion," says Maimonides, "until the pillar of the world, *ammudo shel olam*, our patriarch Abraham, was born." Abraham is the pillar of the world. He is symbolic of balance and support.

A central motif in Judaism emerged with the life story of Abraham. God does not redeem the world or the covenantal community all by Himself; He uses man to perform the great messianic miracle of liberation. God works with instruments. Of course, the whole universe is an instrument in the hands of God, Who created the world in order to realize His inscrutable will through His creatures. However, the most effective tool is man, with his paradoxical characteristics and dialectical nature. God appoints man as His plenipotentiary, His agent, His *shali'ah*. While non-intelligent matter functions mechanically, man acts willfully, intelligently, and freely. Dead, non-intelligent matter cannot choose between obedience and rebellion, whereas man can. Since man can refuse to collaborate with the Almighty, his cooperation is the more welcome.

When God chooses man, He prefers the individual to the multitude. He does not select a group of individuals. Instead, he pulls someone out of the multitude and tells him to be the messenger. The recruitment of sympathizers and friends is the task of the elected individual. This is to demonstrate that the individual is a microcosm, a miniature world provided with all the necessary talents and capacities. Judaism believes that the individual has a universal potential, that he is a creator, a fashioner, an artist who breathes life into the dead and into the cohesive multitude. The individual can spiritually mold the souls and minds of the many. God wants the agent not only to deliver a message but to become a co-redeemer, a fellow creator with Him, so to speak. This is true of the election of the lonely Abraham, segregated from the rest of the world, as well as of Moses, who remained lonely all his life. After all, the Almighty Himself is the Lonely One. His existence is exclusive, negating all others: "Hear, O Israel, the Lord is our God, the Lord is one" (Deut. 6:4), the only one; nothing else exists beside Him. Hence loneliness is bestowed upon the *shali'ah*.

I would go a step further and say that every single individual shares in this loneliness, since it is incumbent upon us to follow in the footsteps of our Maker. A human being should experience loneliness by making sure not to absolutize his bonds with others, even if they are his most intimate friends or the members of his household. There is no prayer without experiencing loneliness. One should be ready when summoned by history to oppose or to reject the status quo, be it cultural or social-political, to answer in the affirmative "*Hinneni*, Here am I." Each individual should possess the strength to pitch his tent on one bank of the river while society lives on the other.

Maimonides wrote that the world moved on in this fashion until Abraham was born. He did not write "until Abraham recognized the Almighty and began to proclaim God's name to the whole world." Apparently, it was immediately with Abraham's birth that the world stopped rushing down into a yawning abyss. The significance of his birth consists in the certitude that greatness in a human being cannot be suppressed or destroyed. No matter how fiendish the circumstances, however corrupt and wicked society may be, genuine holiness and greatness eventually triumph over satanic opposition. Once Abraham was born, it was quite certain that he would redeem the world. The expectation on the part of Providence was that the great courageous spirit which entered the frail body of a crying infant would defy and defeat the power of pagan tyranny.

Interesting is the saying by *Hazal* about the continuity of the Tradition. They tell us, "A righteous person does not depart from the world until another righteous person like him is created. As it is said, 'The sun rises and the sun sets' (Eccl. 1:5)" (*Kiddushin* 72b). *Hazal* speak of birth as a sunrise. Nothing can prevent the rising sun from climbing higher and higher in the sky; nobody can stop the sun from radiating heat and light. In a similar fashion, no society can stop the development and continuous growth of the tiny infant endowed with greatness.

Abraham Finds God

How did Abraham discover God? As a young lad, when he was a shepherd, he used to spend the night in the fields. He could not sleep because he was restless. He could not understand the existence of the cosmos; the grandeur of the cosmic drama puzzled him. He particularly counted the stars. Indeed, Chaldea was the land where astronomy was born. They were the first to describe the skies and draw maps of the heavens. And Abraham discovered God with the stars.

> After this mighty one, *eitan zeh*, was weaned, he began to explore and think, *leshotet be-da'ato*. Although he was a child, he began to think incessantly throughout the day and night, wondering: How is it possible for the sphere to continue to revolve without anyone controlling it? Who makes it revolve? Surely, it does not cause itself to revolve.

> He had no teacher, nor was there anyone to inform him. Rather, he was mired in Ur of the Chaldees among foolish idolaters. His father, mother, and all the people around him were idol-worshippers, and he would worship with them. However, his heart explored and gained understanding.

> Ultimately, he apprehended the way of truth and understood the path of righteousness through his accurate comprehension. He realized that there was one God who controlled the sphere, that He had created everything, and that there is no other God among all the other entities. He knew that the entire world was making a mistake. What caused them to err was their service of the stars and images, which made them lose awareness of the truth. Abraham was forty years old when he became aware of his Creator (*Hilkhot Avodat Kokhavim* 1:3).

Abraham had no teacher. Who then disclosed to him the greatest of all truths, namely, the existence of the Almighty? In fact, God communicated with Abraham constantly, although Abraham was unaware that the intuitive insights and sudden flashes of his mind were words the Almighty addresses to prophets. They constituted a message from the Almighty to him.

We have already established that there are two kinds of prophecy. There is external prophecy, when the prophet beholds a vision or hears a voice coming from the outside. The identity of the speaker is disclosed to the prophet. There is, however, another kind of revelation; it is anonymous. The prophet is unaware of speech coming from beyond; he is not conscious that he is being addressed. The revelation transpires in silence.

This kind of revelation occurred within the great personality of Abraham. God spoke from within. That is why Maimonides emphasizes the fact that Abraham was not instructed by anyone. He was an *eitan,* mighty within himself. The story of Abraham is the story of a gifted and talented child who found the truth all by himself.

An *eitan* has strength that is imperturbable and primeval, an elemental strength upon which many rely and lean. It is the natural and unchangeable strength of the rock. *"Eitan moshavekha,* Your abode is a bulwark, and you have placed your nest in solid rock" (Num. 24:21). The strength of the patriarchs was invincible and unconquerable. Their strength was innate and inseparable from them. Abraham discovered God all by himself. No one taught him, no one guided him. He drew his conclusions from premises his own mind postulated. His knowledge was nurtured by intuitive flashes from within.

In the aggadic literature, there is a controversy concerning the age at which Abraham made the great discovery (Gen. Rabbah 30:8). One rabbi holds that he was three years old, another rabbi that he was forty (or forty-eight) years of age. Maimonides apparently thought that the two opinions are complementary and not contradictory. The search began at an early age—he did not fix the age precisely. However, the discovery or recognition of God occurred later. Maimonides wanted Abraham to spend some forty years searching, exploring, and questing for God. The Mishnah says, *"Ben arba'im le-binah,* At forty, one attains understanding" (*Avot* 5:21). When man is born, he immediately comes in contact with reality. Questing for God is a spontaneous process; not even an infant can forgo this mysterious drive. Yet it takes him forty years before he begins to understand the universe. *Binah* has the connotation of grasping and understanding. Abraham, who began to search for God around the age of three, had to devote some forty years to the bold and heroic enterprise of joining the Infinite.

Maimonides held that questing for God is a spontaneous process. The whole world as an entity is pulled by the Almighty and attracted to Him. Even dead matter, whose motion science has interpreted and formulated in mathematical equations, is driven toward the Creator. The Aristotelian explanation of circular motion, which Maimonides accepted, is completely wrong from a scientific standpoint, but it contains a metaphysico-theological truth. The universe is in physical motion because motion represents a metaphysical quest for the Almighty. Aristotle spoke of four forms of motion which are reducible to two: quantitative locomotion and qualitative morphological motion, or realization of the hyletic. If questing is behind the morphological actualization of all matter, then it is certainly true of human beings, whose development and spiritual growth are to be understood in terms of man's dynamic questing for God. The stronger the yearning, the more intense the search, the quicker and greater the actualization of the hyletic.

While the yearning usually emerges in more advanced developmental stages, Abraham experienced the metaphysical pull very early, at the age of three. On the other hand, to say that Abraham found God or recognized God at that young age would be tantamount to an admission that recognition of God is an easy matter. The Torah in Deuteronomy speaks differently. To find God is a complex, painstaking job that requires unlimited toil and dedication. "And there [in exile] you will seek God, and you will find Him, provided that you inquire with your whole heart and whole soul" (Deut. 4:29). This stipulation can be met only by an adult with a brilliant and fully developed mind, a rich imagination and an extremely sensitive soul. No matter how gifted a child may be, he cannot perform as well as an adult. Hence Maimonides thought that to interpret the Aggadah literally would be wrong. He therefore considered the two opinions not as contradictory but as supplementary. Searching is part of the great, exhilarating, redemptive experience of meeting God. The search began while Abraham was still an infant; the meeting took place decades later.

Creation itself employs motion, the cosmic dynamic, as the medium through which it tries to come closer to God. The same is true of man. He manifests his questing for God through his restlessness, which from time to time results in unwarranted and unjustified nervous physical movement. The urge for God, the will to find Him and be close to Him, appears in the child at a very early age.

During the period of the mother's nursing with her own milk, the child does not see himself as a separate being. He is still a part of the mother just as he was while in the mother's womb, a being inseparable from his mother, nourished and taken care of by her. He is completely dependent upon her. Whatever the age limit of weaning, one thing is obvious: it denotes the first stage of growth of a child, of gaining independence from the mother and recognizing himself as a separate entity and not just a component part of the environment. It is perhaps the most relevant stage of development. As long as Abraham was nursed by his mother, his urge for truth and his inquisitiveness to find the cause behind the cosmic drama were dormant and latent. But after having been weaned from his mother, no matter how small he was—"though he was a child"— the urge was activated.

Leshotet denotes roaming, moving without having a particular place or destination in mind. We see this in a verse in Job. When God asks Satan whence he has come, he answers, "*Mishut ba-aretz u-me-hithallekh bah*, From going to and fro in the earth, and from walking up and down in it" (Job 1:7). He has no definitive objective, no place where he wants to arrive. He wants only to inflict harm, and he can do that anywhere.

There is no doubt that Maimonides had a phrase from Amos in mind when he used this word. He was a great stylist, and many times he coined his own idioms. But he would use a biblical or mishnaic phrase if he could. Amos says "They will travel from sea to sea, from north to east; *yeshotetu*, they will wander about to seek the word of God" (8:12). The child at three, four, or five is restless. He is always on the move, exploring and searching for something. Because the child at this age does not distinguish between reality and fantasy, he is not satisfied with his environment, which is dull and unattractive. He looks for a colorful world and expects to find it either in the woods or in the attic. His imagination is in pursuit of something better and fairer, of something he himself cannot name.

The famous French writer Romain Rolland describes how restless Beethoven was in his youth. From early childhood, Beethoven used to hear melodies. He would say that there was an orchestra hidden somewhere—under the table, behind the curtain, in the attic, or in the oven. He always heard beautiful melodies playing, and he thought it was somewhere outside of himself. The orchestra was indeed an orchestra. But it was hidden in him, not outside of him.

Of course, the more sensitive the child is and the richer his imagination, the bolder he is in his determination to find a different reality. In a word, a child's restlessness represents the spontaneous drive to God that every human being experiences, and which in adults also expresses itself in restlessness. The difference between child and adult consists in the fact that the grown-up experiences the same sense of frustration as Kohelet, his restlessness accompanied by a feeling of futility, while the child does not feel at all frustrated. If he is disappointed, he will try again.

In fact, many children act that way. They certainly possess potential greatness, but their childish cravings are never translated into thought. Their emotional inner storm does not spill over into the cognitive realm, into an experience of intellectual enlightenment; the emotional storm gradually calms without being consummated. The greatness of Abraham consisted in the fact that while he was not encouraged to objectify his emotional agitation in the form of logical categories—on the contrary, he was constantly discouraged—he did succeed in converting volatile primeval emotions into advanced knowledge. He began by being "*meshotet be-da'ato,*" agitated, restless, and then, upon reaching a higher level of intellectual development, he converted this restlessness into thought—"he began to think incessantly throughout the day and night, wondering: How is it possible for the sphere to continue to revolve without anyone controlling it?" He interpreted his longing for something as the quest for God, whom he discovered in both infinity and finitude. His emotions were of an irresistibly compulsive nature.

The restlessness that drove Abraham to inquire and to explore showed up at an early age. However, his agitation and impatience were purely emotional. He acted the way any gifted, sensitive child would have behaved, but his restlessness was not just foam upon the water. It did not disappear with the arrival of maturity. His emotional experience matured with him and turned into an intellectual experience.

There were four basic differences between Abraham's searching and the searching in which other children engage. And since Abraham is the father of our people, not only physically but also spiritually and emotionally, these differences also characterize the unique traits of our historical experience. First, Abraham was persistent. The hostile environment did not nip in the bud his inner activities. He was consistent, almost compulsive. From age three to age forty, he restlessly sought the truth—thirty-seven years! Why didn't he just drop the whole business? The Jew, too, is persistent; in fact, we sometimes act almost compulsively, without rationalizing our commitments. The best example of this is our powerful attachment to *Eretz Yisrael* throughout almost two thousand years of exile. This persistence in the face of the absurd can also be termed faith.

Second, there was continuity between Abraham's experiences. Children usually do not have any sense of continuity. They experience something today, and forget it tomorrow; one minute they are sad, and the next minute happy. Every day, every hour, their world changes, appearing in different colors and shapes. They do not look for a frame of reference or relatedness. But Abraham, even as a child, linked up experiences; his experiences were not abandoned after the stimulation came to an end. He retained them in a living memory, and that is what later helped him develop a new philosophy. The Jew, similarly, is continuity-conscious; his historical awareness is a continuous one. We have a living, warm relationship to the figures and events of our past. This is the essence of our *masorah*, our tradition.

Third, unlike other children, Abraham was searching not for a fantasy world but for reality, true being, for the explanation of cosmic causality and regularity. He possessed a rich imagination, which is the source of creativity, but at the same time he was a realist, concerned with this world. A Jew also has this combination; he is a dreamer and a realist. Jews traditionally were merchants, and no one is more practical than the merchant. Yet the same Jews prayed fervently on Rosh ha-Shanah "that all the inhabitants of the world will recognize and know that to You all knees should be bent"; they dreamt and hoped that the world would be mended under divine rule.

Finally, Abraham searched not only for theory, *noesis*, but for a practical way of life. He rebelled against paganism not only because he resented untruth and erroneous thinking but also for the sake of substituting an ethical life for an immoral one. The Torah hated idolatry because it represented an ugly life, a cruel and vulgar approach to one's fellow man. Abraham fought paganism not only in the name of truth but in the name of justice and kindness to fellow man. He persistently struggled with his environment on behalf of the logos and the ethos. This is what Maimonides means when he says that Abraham "apprehended the way of truth and understood the path of righteousness" (*Hilkhot Avodat Kokhavim* 1:3)—he grasped both the principles of truth and the principles of righteousness or justice, both theory and practice. He preached a new philosophy of monotheism and a new moral code of human dignity, hospitality, and so on. This twin engagement has also characterized the Jew; he has the highest respect for scholarship, for *talmidei hakhamim*, yet also believes that "Study is not the main thing, but practice" (*Avot* 1:17).

Abraham had no transcendental or apocalyptic help in the form of a revelation. God wanted Abraham to discover Him in a natural, normal way. Abraham was extremely talented; he had a profound mind, with an incisive outlook on the world. He was the great critic, the great destroyer, as well as the great builder. He searched for God in silence, without being greeted by the One for whom he was searching and questing. The Almighty told Abraham: If you won't discover Me, there will be no covenantal community. You must discover Me first, by simply mobilizing your own intellect, by watching the world, by observing the cosmos, by introspective reflection and meditation. If you discover Me, then I will reveal Myself.

We can visualize the excitement and the tremor that Abraham experienced when he finally came to the conclusion that there is, behind the millions of stars and flying nebulae, behind the fringes of the orderly and dynamic universe, an omniscient, omnipotent, eternal, and infinite Being Who created all and sustains His creation. Abraham, in a feat of ecstatic joy, in a state of rapture, completely intoxicated with love and longing, would have fallen on his face and fervently prayed. "Dear God, please show me a sign that You are there, beyond everything, outside of time and space. Please reveal Your majesty and splendor. Please say one word to me. Let me hear Your voice. Let me see Your countenance. Let me feel Your breath on my pale fatigued face. Answer me; tell all the pagan idol worshippers that you are the Creator. Lord and Master of the world, come forward; You can make my task so easy and so simple."

However, the Almighty did not respond to Abraham. Abraham encountered an awesome silence, the silence of eternity. The mystery deepened and became more intriguing and frightening. Cynical pagan opponents asked: Why doesn't the Almighty answer you? Why can't He prove His existence to us? However, Abraham was not discouraged. He taught others. He carried the new code of morality selflessly, trying to convert people to the new faith. He exposed himself to the worst of all tortures: ridicule. He believed in an invisible, unapproachable, silent Being. He sacrificed for Him and served Him. He built altars and prayed to Him. The pagans could not grasp it! They ridiculed Abraham's irrational loyalty to God. Their lack of understanding turned into hostility, and they began to persecute Abraham. However, Abraham's faith was not affected by God's silence and transcendence. He served God, teaching and proclaiming a new morality.

🌫 Go Forth from Your Land

God Speaks to Abraham

When Abraham turned seventy-five, decades after he discovered God, he heard the voice of the Almighty for the first time. "And the Lord said to Abram, *Lekh lekha*, Go forth from your land, and from your birthplace, and from your father's house, to the land that I will show you" (Gen. 12:1). According to Nahmanides, we translate *lekh lekha* as "Go forth" and nothing else; there are no semantics to the word; it is simply the idiom. But according to Rashi, the semantics of *lekha* means "for your sake, for your benefit." Migration, moving from place to place, uproots a person and has a negative effect on his renown and wealth. On arriving in the new country, he is a stranger and does not understand the language; he cannot quickly assimilate and adopt its mores and customs. The experience is usually destructive. But in this case, God said, your migration to Canaan will be for your benefit and welfare. There I will make you a great nation—but only there. If you stay here, you will not merit the privilege of having children. Rashi is pointing out that children are a *zekhut,* a special privilege, a divine grace that God bestows upon a father and mother, not something natural that one can simply expect.

Here, indeed, we come across a very strange motif that winds like a scarlet thread through the entire Bible. Beginning with Sarah, the women of the Bible were barren. It took a long time, great effort, many prayers, many sleepless nights, and a lot of despair—and almost resignation—until God granted them a child. People must prove themselves worthy of this gift, and that takes time. God tells Abraham: If you remain in Ur of the Chaldees, you will live in luxury, but not have the greatest of all gifts. Abraham will be worthy of this privilege only in the land of Canaan.

Lekha also speaks of action that is not to be repeated but is final and ultimate. If God had wanted Abraham merely to visit the land of Canaan, He would have said only *"lekh."* But God meant for him to leave the past, to blot out his memory, to emigrate from his country to a new country, and therefore He said, *"lekh lekha."* In the Song of Songs, the Shulammite keeps using different excuses to not join her beloved. Finally, he knocks on her door and says: "Rise up, *kumi lakh*, my love and fair one" (Song 2:10). No more excuses, no apologies. The *lekha* emphasizes the finality of the action. In the *Akedah* story, God tells Abraham, "Take now your son, your only son, Isaac, whom you love, and go, *lekh lekha*, to the land of Moriah" (Gen. 22:2). *Lekha* denotes significance and relevance: the act which is to be done is of great and terrific importance.

A further meaning of *lekh lekha* is "Go alone." God's intent was to separate Abraham, to break up his life and have him forget the past and start anew. The Midrash (Gen. Rabbah 39:1) tells us that when R. Yitzhak read this verse, he always used to cite a verse in Psalms: "Listen, my daughter, and see and give attention, and forget your people and your ancestral home" (Ps. 45:11). He felt that this verse alludes to Abraham. *"Lekh lekha"* commanded a psychological break with Abraham's past, with his ancestral family and tradition. God meant for him to blot out these memories.

The Torah speaks of three departures: physical departure, behavioral departure, and kinship departure (i.e., filial alienation). "Go forth from your land" means simply to emigrate. The addition *mi-moladtekha*, "from your birthplace," is not related to physical emigration, but to departure of another kind, behavioral departure. The early years of our life in our birthplace shape and determine our behavioral patterns, our habits, drives, and desires. The *moledet* can also be understood as the mother, who teaches her child the basics of behavior. "From your father's house" refers to clannish estrangement, alienation from one's kin. Abraham was called upon to form a new fellowship, to forget his past and start life from scratch. In this new fellowship, the teacher becomes the parent and the student becomes the child. A new concept of fatherhood emerged, one based upon communication and common devotion rather than upon biological factors. Parent-teacher and child-disciple relations replace the progenitor-offspring relationship.

Abraham and Terah

Rashi (12:2) emphasizes the breaking of old kinship bonds:

> "[Go forth from] your land"—had he not already departed from there with his father and gone to Haran? Rather, this is what [God] told him: Go still farther away; leave now your father's home also!

Rashi's comment addresses a question that also concerned the Spanish exegetes. Abraham seems to have left Ur of the Chaldees even before the command of *lekh lekha* came to him. Two verses before *lekh lekha* we read:

> And Terah took Abram his son, and Lot the son of Haran his grandson, and Sarai his daughter-in-law, his son

Abram's wife; and they went forth with them from Ur of the Chaldees, to go to the land of Canaan; and they came to Haran, and lived there (Gen. 11:31).

Rashi tries to resolve the difficulty by rearranging the semantics of the verse "Go forth from your land, and from your birthplace, and from your father's house." It seems as if Rashi wants us to place the emphasis upon "your father's house," which was established anew in Haran. The verse, according to Rashi's interpretation, should be understood as follows: "Go forth from your father's house, which was established by Terah in Haran, and by so doing you will remove yourself still further from your land and place of birth (Ur of the Chaldees)."

Ibn Ezra (Gen. 11:31) disagrees with Rashi's interpretation. He says that the Torah does not always follow chronological order. The verse "Go forth" should be integrated after "Sarai was barren; she had no child" (Gen. 11:30). In Ur Sarah is a barren woman, but in Canaan she will give birth to a child. Then "Terah took Abram his son, and Lot the son of Haran his grandson, and Sarai his daughter-in-law, his son Abram's wife; and they went forth with them from Ur of the Chaldees." This was actually in response to the divine command to leave the land of the Chaldees to go to the land of Canaan. There was no reason why Terah should have departed from Ur of the Chaldees. He was a very prominent citizen in Chaldea; he was a member of the royal house and people respected him. Why should a man suddenly emigrate from his native land for no reason under the sun? That is why Ibn Ezra says that Terah went in response to the divine command Abraham received from God.

According to Ibn Ezra, the reconstructed *parashah* would read as follows:

But Sarai was barren; she had no child (Gen. 11:30). And the Lord said to Abram: Go forth from your land, and from your birthplace, and from your father's house, to the land that I will show you. And I will make of you a great nation, and I will bless you, and make your name great; and you shall be a blessing. And I will bless those who bless you, and curse those who curse you; and in you shall all families of the earth be blessed (Gen. 12:1–3). And Terah took Abram his son, Lot the son of Haran his grandson, and his daughter-in-law Sarai his son Abram's wife; and they went forth with them from Ur of the Chaldees to go to the land of Canaan, and they came to Haran, and lived there. And the days of Terah were two hundred and five years; and Terah died in Haran (Gen. 11:31–32). So Abram departed, as the Lord had spoken to him; and Lot went with him; and Abram was seventy-five years old when he departed from Haran (Gen. 12:4).

If we accept this interpretation, we could solve another riddle. Our Sages stated that Terah repented and embraced the new faith his son was preaching (*Midrash Tanhuma, Shemot* 18). They derived this conclusion from the verse "And you shall go to your fathers in peace; you shall be buried in a good old age" (Gen. 15:15). If Terah was the idolater and Abraham was the monotheist, the one who proclaimed the new faith of an invisible single God, how can the verse say that he will join his father in peace? The conclusion to be inferred from this verse is that Terah repented during Abraham's lifetime. However, what we miss is the story of Terah's conversion, the exact moment when Terah realized the futility of an idolatrous life, the absurdity of the entire pagan civilization. When did it happen?

According to the Aggadah, Terah was the one who informed King Nimrod of Abraham's abusive and blasphemous treatment of the hallowed images and idols (Gen. Rabbah 38:13). It was Terah who wanted Abraham the iconoclast to be executed, and he would have succeeded in implementing his fiendish plan if not for the miraculous intervention of the Almighty. Terah bitterly resented Abraham's revolutionary ideas, Abraham's rebellion against society and the established order. Terah so hated Abraham that he denounced him and colluded to have him executed. Later—I don't know how long it took—the same Terah saw the light and realized that Abraham was right and society wrong, that his past was wrong, that a life dedicated to paganism and idolatry, to a cruel philosophy, to ideals in conflict with the basic principles of decency, was a waste. This was a tremendous change in Terah.

What prompted Terah to act so strangely? What motivated him to break up his home, uproot his household, abandon luxury, convenience, renown, influence, and power, and become a wanderer, an immigrant, a straying Chaldean? Surely the great revolution in Terah's thinking was precipitated by doubts, soul-searching, and reappraisal. In a word, it was the transvaluation of a *ba'al teshuvah* that was responsible for the decision to abandon Ur in Chaldea and start out for a primitive land where he planned to begin a new life.

God commanded Abraham to emigrate from Ur of the Chaldees after Terah had undergone the great, dramatic change and had decided to give up everything and go forth to a new world. Whether Terah knew of Abraham's rendezvous with God in the fertile fields of Chaldea under the starry night sky is hard to ascertain. Equally difficult to answer is the question of whether Abraham ever told Terah about the instructions he received from God pertaining to the journey to an unknown country. However, all that is irrelevant. What is important is the coincidence of revelation and free decision. When the command of *lekh lekha* came and Abraham began to pack his bags, he realized to his great surprise that his father's bags had already been packed long before. Father and son, hitherto locked in mortal combat, joined hands and together started out on the great march to Canaan, away from the hustling and bustling cities of Chaldea, away from a highly developed country, away from a magical, well-organized, and disciplined social order.

Nahmanides (Gen. 12:1) challenges the position taken by Ibn Ezra:

> But this is not correct, for if so, it would follow that Abram was the central figure in the journey from his father's house by command of God, while Terah his father voluntarily went with him. Yet Scripture says, "And Terah took Abram his son" (11:31), which teaches us that Abram followed his father and that it was by his counsel that Abram went forth from Ur of the Chaldees.

I believe that the question can be easily resolved. The Torah is more interested in the metamorphosis that Terah experienced than in Abraham's compliance with the word of God. The greatest story of a *ba'al teshuvah* is told in the verse "And Terah took"—the spontaneous decision to abandon everything he had loved and defended, the change from an idolater into a member of Abraham's fellowship. His emigration from Ur of the Chaldees is a great epic about which the Torah tells us but a few words. Abraham emerged victorious; he convinced his own father.

Maimonides' position is that the fact that a parent is immoral should not affect the child's attitude. Even if one's mother and father are rotten through and through, one is supposed to give them respect and revere them (*Hilkhot Mamrim* 6:11). Abraham came to Terah and entrusted the divine command to him, and took him into his confidence. Terah apparently responded with zeal, so Abraham immediately realized that Terah was in a process of changing, that Terah was abandoning not only the physical city of Ur of the Chaldees, but also its ideals, observances, mores, and customs. Since he felt obligated to give him respect and to revere him, he made it appear to outsiders that the one who had taken the initiative was not himself but Terah.

We have forgotten how to respect father and mother. Of course, *kibbud av* expresses itself in helping one's parents. If they are poor, we must give them a stipend. If they are frail, we must help them get into their overcoats or take them for a drive on a nice day. But this is not the Jewish *kibbud av*; this is Esau's *kibbud av*. Isaac was hungry, so Esau cooked a tasty meal for him. Physical service is important, but is only of peripheral importance; what is important is the mental attitude.

First of all, one must be polite and protect one's parent from being hurt, from feeling humiliated, from insults and abuses. It is very easy for an elderly person to feel insulted. He is sensitive, sometimes overly so. Abraham was careful not to have Terah think that Abraham was now the head of the family, so he arranged matters in such a way that everyone who saw them making arrangements and preparations thought it was Terah's decision. Terah was the central figure; he gave the orders and led the caravan. Abraham remained in the background. The Torah does not describe the events as they really took place— with Abraham as the mover, the director, the manager, the person to whom the word of God was addressed and the one who made the family emigrate from Ur of the Chaldees—because the Torah is interested in Abraham's actions serving for us as a model of behavior. Jewish history is a history of morality, of a personification of ideals. It is important for us to know the way Abraham conducted himself vis-à-vis his father.

Terah felt the mysterious pull that the Holy Land exerted upon those who search for meaning and a rationale in life and who are questing for God. "For that was his intention, as well as that of his father when they originally set forth from Ur of the Chaldees" (Nahmanides, Gen.12:1). But, of course, in spite of his good intentions, in spite of his penitential mood and his courage to leave home for a distant land, Terah did not succeed. He did not reach the destination; he settled in Haran and died there. Abraham continued the march to the land of Canaan and implemented the vision. In spite of the change that occurred in him, Terah did not succeed in transforming himself totally. He still had his fears and doubts. He fluctuated and was unsure of himself. He lacked the heroic quality his son possessed. He did not know the response of *"Hinneni*, I am here."

The Souls That They Had Made in Haran

Abraham set out with his wife, his nephew, their possessions, "and the souls that they had made in Haran" (Gen. 12:5). Targum Yerushalmi (Pseudo-Yonatan) translates this phrase as *"ve-yat nafshata di gayru be-Haran."* Like the Midrash and Rashi, he refers to those who had been converted. Targum Onkelos uses a different phrase, *"ve-yat nafshata de-sha'avidu le-Oraita be-Haran."* Why didn't he use the simpler term *de-gayru*?

We know that conversion requires acceptance of the yoke of the commandments, plus immersion in a mikveh and circumcision. In fact, immersion and circumcision are technical media, but the essence of conversion expresses itself in the unconditional and total commitment to fulfill the *mitzvot*. Of course, conversion requires both strict observance and the convert's involvement with heart and soul in the historical destiny of the Jewish people. He must share the travail, the misery, and the worry. The prototype of the convert is Ruth, who said *"Ammekh ammi*, your people shall be my people, *ve-Elokayikh Elokai*, and your God my God" (Ruth 1:16). Abraham did not have yet *mitzvot* to suggest to converts, but he had already tasted what it means to be lonely, and the converts had to accept that. Certainly, it was *ammekh ammi* to abandon one's home and wander with Abraham to a new land.

However, I think *de-sha'avidu le-Oraita* does not refer to this. When God speaks of Abraham, He doesn't speak only in terms of an abstract religious experience. "For I know him, that he will command his children and his household after him, and they shall keep the way of the Lord to do *tzedek u-mishpat*, righteousness and judgment" (Gen. 18:19). Apparently,

Abraham's faith in God was not simply abstract faith. It resulted in a commitment to *tzedek u-mishpat*. There was hospitality,
sympathy, compassion, the readiness to fight for justice and
defend it. This is exactly what the converts had to accept. One
who believes in God must be merciful and understanding, toler-
ant and charitable, ready to defend the weak and the helpless.
Abraham did not have the system of *mitzvot bein adam la-
Makom*, commandments regulating relations between man and
God, but he had an ethical system that had to be carried out and
implemented. That is what Targum Onkelos means by saying
de-sha'avidu le-Oraita—they committed themselves. Conversion
always means a commitment additional to that which every
member of the human family is obligated to fulfill. *Tzedakah* is
not included in the Noahide laws; *tzedakah* is Abraham's
domain.

Rashi (12:5) comments on "that they made in Haran" as
"*she-hikhnisam tahat kanfei ha-Shekhinah*, they brought them
under the wings of the *Shekhinah*." This is an expression which
Hazal used time and again when they wanted to say conversion
plain and simple. It is a metaphor that means providing protection and shelter. God is described in Psalms as the one who
gives us shelter: "God is my *sela*, my rock" (Ps. 18:3; see also
31:4, 42:10 and 71:3). I will tell you frankly, it was only when I
went to *Eretz Yisrael* that I realized immediately why God is
called *sal'i*. In *Eretz Yisrael*, particularly the Negev, where it is
completely desert and the heat is insufferable, we can see a
Bedouin shepherd and his flock clinging to a rock. The rock
casts a shadow, and they find shelter in its shadow. This is
Hashem sal'i. A shadow gives shelter when the blazing sun is at
its zenith. God is the shade in which one finds shelter and
peace. *Sal'i* does not mean hard or tough like a rock; that would
not be a proper description of the Creator.

A person without God, a person who denies God or negates
Him, who drifts from Him or is alienated from Him—such a person is homeless and uprooted. He can never rest or enjoy peace

of mind. He never has a feeling of security, no matter how powerful or wealthy he may be. There is an inner sense of insecurity and other frights, a variety of phobias and fears that befall him and take possession of every fiber of his soul. Complete security and peace, full harmony and serenity can be found only in God. That is why the *Shekhinah* is like two large wings that cast shade, and in that shade a person finds a cool place and protection against the heat, against fatigue and exhaustion, against desolation and loneliness. Modern man has been alienated from God for so long; he is like a leaf carried by the wind, uprooted completely. But when he is *tahat kanfei ha-Shekhinah* he is very close to God. "The Lord is near to all those who call upon him" (Ps. 145:18). "Seek the Lord while he may be found; call upon him while he is near" (Isa. 55:6). *Tahat kanfei ha-Shekhinah* has the connotation of restfulness, peace, serenity, rootedness and being anchored—the opposite of the feeling of homelessness. Man becomes a resident of a certain place; otherwise he is a vagabond in this world. "I have been a stranger" (Ex. 2:22). One can establish a residence only when one is close to God.

There is a natural desire, a natural yearning in every human being, Jew and gentile alike, who all were created in the image of God, to come as close as possible to the Master of the Universe. The *Tanya* (*Likkutei Amarim*, chaps. 12, 19, 38) calls this drive *ahavah tiv'it*, the natural love for God—and not only for God, but for everything that is good and noble and sacred. Of course, we find wicked people who like the vulgar, the brazen, and the ugly. But this is either because they repress the drive for the beautiful and for God, or because they are not cognizant of it due to the environment or friends who smother the still, small voice of the human personality.

But, as Maimonides says, "The Torah has already promised that ultimately Israel will repent" (*Hilkhot Teshuvah* 7:5). *Teshuvah* is not only a duty, not only an obligation, not only a command; it is also a promise by God that in the end *Keneset*

Yisrael as a whole will come back to God. No matter how alienated she has been, no matter how far she has removed herself from God, no matter how deeply she is immersed in sin, vulgarity, and iniquity, she will come back, as it says: "And it shall come to pass, when all these things have come upon you, the blessing and the curse . . . and you shall return to the Lord your God" (Deut. 30:1–2). According to Maimonides, this is not a mitzvah, but rather a promise that willy-nilly the Jewish people will return to God.

The deep-seated human yearning for God can never be repressed fully. An individual can sometimes repress this yearning not only when young but even in old age. Some people are cowards and are afraid to change and amend their ways because this would mean alienation of friends and family. But, basically, there is in everyone *hirhur teshuvah*, a natural yearning to return to God. The psalmist says, "As the hind longs for water brooks, so does my soul long for you, O God" (Ps. 42:2). When a human being is thirsty, he knows that he is thirsty, and finding water is a conscious activity, an intentional, purposefully motivated act. But when the animals in the jungles of Africa walk toward water, they are not conscious of why they are going. Of course, they move on until they reach the water, but they are driven by a mechanical, indomitable, irresistible urge to stoop and drink. That is the way man is sometimes driven to God. He is pushed, just as the animal is pushed "for water streams."

Kedushah fascinates; man in all his aspirations, hopes, visions, dreams, and yearning is out to realize the idea of holiness, to find God and cling to him. *Kedushah* has a strange quality; it frightens people, but it also pulls and attracts them. It is daunting with regard to those who refuse to think, to feel, to delve within themselves, to understand the mystery of man and his strange destiny. However, for those blessed with sweep of imagination, depth of perception, breadth of thought, and boldness of character, *kedushah* is the most fascinating experience, pulling them unconsciously and instinctually to the Creator. At times, it is hard to protect oneself against the onslaught of *kedushah*; it is hard to run away from the Creator, who trails behind man and challenges him to come back.

Abraham Reaches Shechem

We must not imagine that Abraham left Haran in the morning and arrived in Canaan in the afternoon. Instead, he wandered from one place to another, exploring many countries, wondering whether or not he had found the land of which the Almighty had spoken. Abraham himself said, "And it came to pass, when God *hit'u oti* from my ancestral home"— *hit'u oti* means that God caused me to wander, to be lost, to go astray (Gen. 20:13). Abraham did not say "when God told me to go to Canaan." In fact, when God commanded Abraham to depart from his ancestral home, He did not mention the destination to which Abraham was supposed to proceed. He was to go "to the land that I will show you" (Gen. 12:1). Apparently, many a time Abraham felt lost, but God did not say a single word. Abraham himself had to identify the place; no help was offered. "A wandering Aramean was my father [Abraham]" (cf. Rashbam, Deut. 26:5).

"And Abram passed through the land unto the place of Shechem . . . and the Lord appeared to Abraham and said: To your seed will I give this land; and he built there an altar unto the Lord who appeared to him" (Gen. 12:6–7). Why was it necessary to say "who appeared to him"? The sentence "He built there an altar to the Lord" would have sufficed. The answer is clear. He built the altar because God had confirmed his choice of the land by appearing to him. Abraham knew that his intuitive choice was correct, and he built an altar to the Lord, who had appeared to him and sanctioned his choice of the land.

Rashi (Gen. 12:2) says, "He did not reveal the land to him immediately, in order to make it precious in his eyes," and notes in the same comment, "Similarly we find [in Gen. 22:2], 'upon one of the mountains which I shall tell you.' " When Abraham was commanded to offer Isaac on Mount Moriah, God did not identify the mountain on whose top the sacrifice was to take place. Abraham had to search for the mountain and identify it intuitively; only then would God confirm it. The Bible tells us that it took Abraham three days to find and recognize the mount (Gen. 22:4). He found it, and God sanctioned his finding. "And they came to the place of which God told him" (Gen. 22:9). However, prior to the word of God confirming the identity of the place, Abraham had to find it by himself. King David and the Sanhedrin searched long and hard and decided in favor of Ornan's threshing floor as the site for the Temple. Only afterwards did God sanction their choice through the prophet Gad. "Then the angel of the Lord commanded Gad to say to David that David should go up and rear an altar to the Lord in the threshing floor of Ornan the Jebusite" (I Chron. 21:18). First one must search for the abode; only then will one be able to establish the sanctuary.

Here is a central idea in Judaism: *kedushah* attracts. This was perhaps the greatest discovery made by Abraham. The generation of the flood thought that beauty is fascinating and that it man's duty of to respond quickly to the aesthetic challenge, to succumb to the beautiful and pleasant. The generation of the dispersion thought that power is the idea that overwhelms man; technological achievement takes man prisoner, making him worship the genius who made this kind of achievement possible. Abraham proclaimed to the world that *kedushah* is the great attractive force.

The Almighty has implanted in the Jew a sensitivity to *kedushah*, to the holy. We are supposed to react to *kedushah* the way the eye reacts quickly and sharply to a beam of light. In a word, the covenantal community is supposed to be equipped with a sixth sense enabling it to be spontaneously attracted by the holy and to discriminate between the holy and the profane. Abraham was tested to determine whether or not he possessed the capability. His whole destiny was dependent upon the out-come of these tests, and he came out with flying colors. He iden-tified *kedushah* even though others, who saw just the surface, did not recognize the mount (Gen. Rabbah 56:2). Knowledge of God is not just abstract in nature. It is dynamic, passionate, experiential, all-powerful, and all-redeeming. It is not knowl-edge in the ordinary sense of the word; it is ecstatic and per-ceptional.

Abraham entered Canaan from the north, the most fertile part of the country. Abraham was a shepherd; he needed land for pasture. Why didn't he settle in one of the northern valleys? Rashi (Gen. 12:9) raised the question, and answered that Abraham was moving toward Jerusalem, which is in the south-ern belt of Canaan. The holiness of Jerusalem pulled him instinctively toward the south. Abraham was instinctively attracted by *kedushah* the way the bee is attracted by the nec-tar of the flower.

Praying at Shechem

Interestingly, the Torah uses the phrase "*mekom Shechem*, the place of Shechem" and not "*ir Shechem*, the city of Shechem," as it did with regard to Jacob: "And Jacob came to the city of Shechem, which is in the land of Canaan" (Gen. 33:18). *Makom*, with regard to the patriarchs, means a place for prayer: "And he lighted upon a certain place, *va-yifga ba-makom*, and remained there all night" (Gen. 28:11). Based on this verse, *Hazal* say that Jacob was the one who established the evening prayers (*Berakhot* 26b). He petitioned God *ba-makom*, at a certain place. Prayer requires a set place—one should designate a place for prayer (*Berakhot* 6b). A *beit keneset* is sacred because prayer is inseparably combined and intertwined with *makom*, with place. "Abraham went early in the morning to the place, *makom*, where he stood before the Lord" (Gen. 19:27)—the place, the *makom*, where he was confronted by God, where he encountered the Almighty and stood with Him face to face. *Hazal* say this is the morning prayer, because *tefillah* means being confronted by God the way we confront someone else and engage him in a conversation, in a dialogue, face to face (*Berakhot* 26b).

This association here of *makom* with *mekom tefillah* is the motivation of *Hazal*'s comment (cited by Rashi to Gen. 12:6), " 'Abram came *ad mekom Shechem*'—to pray for the sons of Jacob when they engaged in combat in Shechem" when Dina was dishonored. Shechem wanted to impose upon them complete integration and assimilation, "Give your daughters to us and take our daughters for you" (Gen. 34:9). If they had not engaged Shechem in combat, *Keneset Yisrael* would have disappeared long ago. Abraham was the personification and the epitome of *hesed*. But at certain times a person cannot just follow that principle. When he confronts evil, when he confronts a fiend who is ready to exterminate and destroy, he should be capable of fighting. Otherwise he cannot exist. Shechem was a question of survival for the Jews—either to survive as the community Abraham has founded and was destined for a great task—*le-goy gadol*—or to disappear and be wiped off the map. That is why they fought; they could not help themselves. Of course, to win a war requires the element of surprise—this is a decisive factor.

The crime was committed by only one individual, Shechem ben Hamor, but apparently the brothers considered the entire town to be hostile to the household of Jacob. If one commits a crime and the community does not ostracize him, or if one preaches bigotry and hatred and the community does not condemn him, isolate him, or try to eliminate him, then a conspiracy of silence is just as bad as a conspiracy of action. As Maimonides says, "It is for this reason that all the males of Shechem were deserving of death, for Shechem abducted and they saw and knew, yet they did not bring him to justice" (*Hilkhot Melakhim* 9:14).

Abraham went "*ad mekom Shechem ad Elon Moreh*" (Gen. 12:6). Rashi says that Shechem and Elon Moreh are two names of the place next to Mount Gerizim and Mount Ebal, where the oaths were to be taken in the future. "You shall put the blessing upon Mount Gerizim, and the curse upon Mount Ebal. Are they not on the other side of the Jordan, by the way where the sun goes down, in the land of the Canaanites . . . beside Elonei Moreh?" (Deut. 11:29–30). At Shechem, Abraham prayed for the Jew to be triumphant in warfare, in his physical engagement. Abraham also prayed for the Jew to emerge victorious from his spiritual engagement with life, so as to be able to realize and implement the oath taken at Mount Gerizim and Mount Ebal. The oath did not revolve about warfare; it revolved about individual sacrifice, about the determination of the Jew to hand down the heritage from generation to generation.

Sometimes, someone who is ready to sacrifice himself and bring the supreme sacrifice on the field of battle is not ready to sacrifice some forbidden desire, physiological drive, or physiological pressure. Heroism on the field of battle is a very glamorous and spectacular heroism. But there is another heroism which is not public. Most *mitzvot* concern one's private life. No one watches; there are no onlookers. It is just a relationship between oneself and God. This is a heroism which does not revolve around outstanding acts, victories in, battle, or destroying air forces, but is about defeating oneself.

"Not with you alone will I make this covenant and this oath. But with he who stands here with us this day before the Lord our God, and also with he who is not here with us this day" (Deut. 29:13–14). This covenant has been made with every individual throughout Jewish history. No matter how many millennia separate a Jew from the ceremony on Mount Gerizim and Mount Ebal, every Jew is burdened with an oath to implement that covenant. Abraham prayed for this oath to be implemented and for the Jews to have the strength, courage, and fortitude to carry on.

Faith is the ability to defy laughter, to defy cynical scoffing, to defy opposition, to defy enmity and hostility and to believe in something that on the surface seems nonsensical and absurd.

The Canaanites were a tall, muscular people. How could Abraham conquer the land and take it away from these giants? Abraham came to Shechem, the metropolitan capital city of the Canaanites. He saw there people "whose height was like the height of the cedars and who were strong as the oaks" (Amos 2:9). It was here that God told him that the land would belong to him. Is there a greater absurdity? But there he built an altar to God.

From Shechem, Abraham moved "to a mountain in the east of Beth-El, and pitched his tent, having Beth-El on the west, and Ai on the east" (Gen. 12:8). Rashi comments that he foresaw that his children would stumble in that area when Joshua conquered the Land of Israel. Joshua had consecrated the booty of Jericho to God, and Achan succumbed to temptation and stole from the booty. Because of that sin, the Jews lost the battle with Ai. It was the only battle in which Joshua was defeated by the enemy.

Interestingly, when Rashi speaks about Shechem, he says that Abraham petitioned God to help his children when they engaged the residents of Shechem in battle. Here Rashi does not say that Abraham offered a prayer for his children when they attacked the people of Ai. His offspring lost the battle; thirty-six Jews were killed and the enemy emerged victorious from that battle (Joshua 7:5), but there was no prayer offered by Abraham. He did not intercede with the Almighty there because he considered the defeat to be deserved by *Benei Yisrael*.

God punished the entire community, even though not a single Jew had helped Achan! However, they forgot that every individual must consider himself responsible for the entire community. On the day the Jews became a political nation, when they crossed the Jordan River and got their own territory, the concept of *arevut*, responsibility, was disclosed to them. Every Jew was responsible for the community, and the community for every individual Jew.

The catastrophes in the twentieth century were due to irresponsibility on the part of decent people who simply kept quiet when wicked people began to preach immorality and crime and hatred and bigotry. That happened in Germany with Hitler. Not every German was a Nazi. I lived in Germany for many years; there were decent people there. I never encountered a single incident of antisemitism at the university in a relationship between professor and student or between students. But they tolerated Hitler, and he finally converted the entire nation into a nation of Nazis. Abraham's doctrine taught that evil is not to be tolerated.

Building an Altar

"And the Lord appeared to Abram, and said, To your seed will I give this land; and there he built an altar to the Lord who appeared to him" (Gen. 12:7). Abraham built an altar, but he did not offer anything on it. The altar itself was a symbol of his submission and surrender to God, and of his complete, unlimited, boundless faith in the Creator. It was the highest form of sacrifice—the sacrifice of his pride, his vanity, his sense of independence.

The altar was also an expression of Abraham's gratitude to God. He was grateful for two things, says Rashi. First, that he would be blessed with offspring, because "Sarai was barren; she had no child" (Gen. 11:30). This was the first time he heard from God that he was going to be the father of children. Second, he was told that the land would be his. Until now God had never promised that *Eretz Yisrael* would be granted to him or to his children. The first time he encountered the Almighty, "The Lord said to Abram: Go forth from your land, and from your birthplace, and from your father's house, to the land that I will show you. And I will make of you a *goy gadol*, a great nation" (Gen. 12:1–2). Apparently, Abraham understood that he would be a great nation not through posterity related to him biologically, but through converts, a faith community that he would found. According to the Jewish view, the teacher is the father of the pupil. He has a share in the pupil as much as a parent has in his child.

Now Abraham realized that God meant "I will make of you a great nation" in a natural way. Of course, Abraham did not give up on the idea of converting the world. He saw no conflict or contradiction between this and his original dream; he still thought it was his mission to teach the world. His son would also be his pupil. He taught Isaac, he trained and developed him. The ideal parent-child relationship is expressed not through a biological link, but through spiritual adherence and communication. "*Avraham holid et Yitzhak*, Abraham fathered Isaac" (Gen. 25:19). The term *holid*, which *prima facie* is semantically and etymologically restricted to the natural relationship, is used to denote the activity of the teacher. "And Joseph saw Ephraim's children of the third generation, the children also of Machir the son of Manasseh were brought up (*yulledu*) upon Joseph's knees" (Gen. 50:23). Joseph brought them up, he taught and trained them.

Abraham's sacrifice may have an additional meaning. Note that the verse adds two words which at first glance seem to be superfluous: "There he built an altar to the Lord *ha-nir'eh elav*, who appeared to him." Abraham felt grateful and indebted to God simply for the fact that He had searched him out, contacted him, and engaged him in a dialogue—simply because of the relationship between him and the Master of the Universe. Until now, apparently, Abraham had never encountered God. Nahmanides (Gen. 12:7) says that the instruction *lekh lekha* was a command, but there was not the full experience of meeting God and of having a rendezvous with Him. God is now *ha-nir'eh elav*, He who revealed Himself to him, who is now his companion. Finally, after living through the experience of loneliness, where sometimes it seemed as if God did not answer his prayers, Abraham found God, in whose name he had been speaking for such a long time, whose laws he had been teaching, whose morality he had been disseminating. That is why Abraham was grateful. That is why he offered a sacrifice of thanks and gratitude.

Nahmanides offers an additional explanation: "It may be that *ha-nir'eh eilav* hints at the mystery of *korban, ve-hamaskil yavin.*" This latter phrase means that whoever is acquainted with *hokhmat ha-Kabbalah*, with mysticism, will understand what he means. Nahmanides, at the beginning of Leviticus (1:9), writes that when the Torah uses the word *korban*, it means human sacrifice and not that of an animal. The Torah, of course, abhors and rejects human sacrifice—but only as far as its physical implementation is concerned. Man belongs to God. All our possessions, all our talents, all our thoughts, all our feelings—everything belongs to God. There is not a single thing in human life which does not belong to Him. There is not a single thing which God does not want man to offer Him, including man himself, including his own existence. An animal is a very inadequate substitute for the real and genuine *korban*, which is human sacrifice. Yet the Torah says that man can substitute something else for his own being. What the Torah is really out to achieve, of course, is observance of all the *mitzvot*. God is interested not so much in human sacrifice as in human restraint, human control, human surrender, human submission. If man is ready to sacrifice his life, and spiritually surrenders to God, then he can bring a substitute for himself. God knows man, his frailties, his weaknesses, his indecision, and his self-love; and because of His compassion, His *middat ha-rahamim*, God substituted animal sacrifice for human sacrifice. R. Shimon ben Azzai observed that whenever the Torah speaks of *korban* there is no mention of *E-l* or *Elokim*; only *Hashem*, the Tetragrammaton, is mentioned (*Menahot* 110a). The Tetragrammaton means *rahamim*, mercy. If God dealt with man in accordance with strict justice, He would require of man—himself.

This is the story of the *Akedah*. There was no need to test Abraham; God knew very well who he was. God wanted Abraham to bring Isaac because God wants everything from man, including the most cherished possession man has. And Abraham surrendered Isaac.

Let us look at the verses in the *Akedah* story. "*Ha-Elokim* tested Abraham" (Gen. 22:1). Abraham "went to the place of which *ha-Elokim* had told him" (Gen. 22:3). He tells Isaac that "*Ha-Elokim* will Himself provide a lamb" (Gen. 22:8). "They came to the place which *ha-Elokim* had told him . . . and Abraham stretched out his hand, and took the knife to slay his son. And the angel of *Hashem* called to him from heaven" (Gen. 22:9–11). The angel says, "Now I know that you fear *Elokim*" (Gen. 22:12). "And Abraham lifted up his eyes . . . And Abraham called the name of that place *Hashem yir'eh*" (Gen. 22:13–14). "And the angel *Hashem* called to Abraham from heaven the second time" (Gen. 22:15). Why are names changed throughout this story?

Elokim is always *middat ha-din*, strict justice—no pardon, no mercy, no *hesed*. As long as strict justice prevails and the *middat ha-din* rules in the world, man has no substitute for *korban*, he has to offer himself. Of course, it was much harder for Abraham to offer Isaac than to offer himself; indeed, God demanded Isaac because he was more precious to Abraham than his own life. We can imagine Abraham's desolation and loneliness. He knew that on the way back there would be no Isaac. He knew this was the last journey with Isaac. In a matter of days, Isaac would be gone and Abraham would travel alone. There would be no more companionship, no more young child in the house, no more laughter, no more enjoyment, no more joy. This was the *korban*, and God was satisfied. When Abraham approached the altar, God said, Now I just want a substitute, a symbol, because you have already surrendered your son. "Abraham went and took the ram, and offered him up for a burnt offering in place of his son" (Gen. 22:13). The idea of substitution thereby came into Judaism. God's name changed from *Elokim* to *Hashem.*

Abraham was a *yerei Elokim*, one who fears *Elokim*, when his relationship with God was one of strict justice, of total surrender, when God wanted him to give away the best he had. It is easy to be a *yerei Hashem* when God treats you with love, charity, and kindness, when He bestows grace and benevolence upon you like a father treats his son. But to be *yerei Elokim* when God applies *middat ha-din*, the measure of justice, when you have to surrender everything and to thank Him for hardships, is very difficult. "Now I know that you fear *Elokim*, seeing that you did not withhold your son, your only son, from Me" (Gen. 22:12).

Later we read, "And I appeared to Abraham, to Isaac, and to Jacob by the name of God Almighty, but by My name *Hashem* I was not known to them" (Ex. 6:3). With regard to Abraham, I did not reveal the *middat ha-rahamim*; I was very strict with him, I tested him so many times, and I demanded from him his own son. I did not reveal myself to Abraham at the very beginning as a merciful God, full of kindness, benevolence, and charity—and therefore not wanting anything from man. Rather, I wanted everything from him.

Abraham built an altar to *Hashem ha-nir'eh eilav*. True, it was *Hashem* guiding him; however, Abraham perceived Him not as *Hashem* but as the King of justice. It was to this exacting and demanding God, *ha-nir'eh eilav*, that Abraham built an altar. Abraham did not sacrifice an animal because *ha-nir'eh eilav* rejected animal sacrifices. Animal sacrifice is merely a substitute for the genuine sacrifice, and for that we need a special dispensation from God—when He changes His name from *Elokim* to *Hashem*. When Abraham arrived in *Eretz Yisrael,* God guided him and treated him not with the *shem Hashem*, the Tetragrammaton, but with the *shem Elokim*. Abraham did not offer a sacrifice because he knew what was really expected of him. He anticipated a command from God to place *himself* upon the altar. The command finally came: Abraham was not to put himself upon the altar. It was a much harder request, one almost impossible to comply with—to offer his only son. Without *shem Hashem*, all sacrifices demand the ultimate offering. This is the mystery hinted at by *ha-nir'eh eilav*.

✒ *A Wandering Aramean*

The Hagirah *Commandment*

The narrative about Abraham's life begins with the *hagirah* commandment to go forth from his land and paternal home to parts unknown. This departure from an indigenous environment and ancestral home to a strange land marks the turning point in Abraham's career, his election to head the paradoxical covenantal community, the bestowal upon him of charismatic uniqueness. God, addressing Himself later to Abraham and offering him the covenant we call the *berit bein ha-betarim,* introduces Himself as the one who started him on his journey: "I am the Lord who brought you out of Ur of the Chaldees to give you this land to inherit it" (Gen. 15:7). We are impressed by the frequent recurrence of the nomadic motif, the destiny of wandering forth, of deserting old native surroundings, of straying in strange places along uncharted lanes, of being lost in foreign lands, of exploring the unknown, the new, the strange. This is a central theme in the life stories of our patriarchs and especially in that of Abraham.

Even after his arrival in Canaan, Abraham moved from place to place. He even had to spend some time in Egypt. Isaac was not allowed to leave the promised land, but he wandered from place to place within the borders of the holy land. Jacob, as is self-evident, was the exile *par excellence*. Indeed, one of the symbolic actions which has influenced the unfolding of our historical drama is the "wandering" of our forefathers. Nahmanides (Gen. 12:1) employs, with reference to Abraham, a phrase of the psalmist, "They wandered from one nation to another and from one kingdom to another people" (Ps. 105:13). He apparently used this verse because we Jews have been wandering throughout our history from nation to nation, from people to people, and from kingdom to kingdom. We knocked on the doors of many kingdoms; some opened their doors to us, some didn't.

The order addressed to Abraham in Ur of the Chaldees did not entail any specifics. Abraham testifies, "And it came to pass when God caused me to go astray" (Gen. 20:13). Nahmanides emphasizes that Abraham was as perplexed as a straying sheep. God did not guide Abraham. He bewildered him; He completely mystified and confounded him. He told him to move on, to go forth "to the land which I will show you." Is the land to be found in the east or the west? No hint was disclosed to Abraham. God willed Abraham to guess, to find out intuitively, to somehow smell the fragrance of the land, to feel the pull that the land exerts, to be attracted by the land spontaneously, so that the heart was Abraham's compass or lodestar. If Abraham had been mistaken in his adventurous selection of the land, everything would have been lost; Abraham would not have been the charismatic chosen leader and patriarch.

The exodus from Chaldea presented Abraham with the crucial challenge or test of whether he was worthy of the divine charisma. God demanded it because history quite often demands of us resolute action and bold choices among equally attractive and appealing alternatives, forcing us to rely solely on intuitive thinking. We often reach a major decision, a most critical judgment, not by thinking out logically the pros and the cons but by listening to our heart. God wanted Abraham to set the example.

Inner and Outer Galut

Galut—exile—burst forth and converged upon man with the first commission of sin. Man lost his existential place and sense of security, and became cognizant of being uprooted and homeless. He anticipated his own extinction and felt that with every passing second he was getting closer and closer to that awesome and grisly destination. "God exiled him from the paradise" (Gen. 3:23).

Banishment must not necessarily be understood in a geographic sense, as if one were banished from a definite spot into some hitherto unknown territory. True, *galut* is a curse if it is experienced literally as geographic dislocation, as forced departure from one's home or native land. Yet *galut* can also refer to being banished from oneself, being exiled from a true and full existence, being tossed by the winds of "accident," being burdened with a sick anguish in one's heart.

Galut as an inner experience is constructive and redeeming. It frees us from absurd vanity and foolish haughtiness. This exile awareness is *per se* redemptive, because man seeks shelter and serenity in God in answer to the grisly fright of nihility. The quest for God is precipitated by the utter despair that follows upon being abandoned by God. The dread of confronting nihility challenges sedate and self-righteous man and drives him to rise. Exile is the prologue to return.

When the Torah enjoined us against succumbing to self-glorification and insolent pride, it emphasized our human helplessness and wretchedness.

> Take care lest you forget the Lord your God. . . . When you have eaten your fill and built fine houses to live in, and your herds and flocks have multiplied, and your silver and gold have increased, and everything you own has prospered, beware lest your heart grow haughty and you forget the Lord your God . . . and you say to yourselves, "My own power and the might of my own hand have won this wealth for me" (Deut. 8:11–14, 17).

Only through the awareness of exile—of the insecurity, alienation, and absurdity of human existence—can man return to the God who helps him to be redeemed from this tragic awareness. If man lives through the dark night of an exiled, frightened soul which purges him of all pride, megalomania, and sickly haughtiness, there is no need for him to be banned from his physical home. He will have tasted the ordeal of spiritual-metaphysical homelessness.

Our patriarchs' frequent travels and changes of residence are considered by Nahmanides as the anticipatory signs portending *galut* on a national scale, the most bitter and tragic experience of our history. Yet the word *galut* lends itself to a number of interpretations; it is a poly-semantic term. When God in His inscrutable wisdom decrees that exile be experienced, the experiential exile of the soul is a genuine substitute for that physical banishment. The Midrash says that we were commanded to dwell in *sukkot* for seven days because dwelling in the *sukkah* is a substitute for the physical exile to which we might have been sentenced on Yom Kippur (*Yalkut Shim'oni, Emor*, 653, quoted in *Sha'arei Teshuvah, Orah Hayyim* 625:1). The Midrash is not referring to the physical inconvenience but to the inner experience of *Sukkot*, which revolves about the experiential homelessness of man, his exposure to the immanent destructive forces of nature.

Disengagement as a Theme in Prophecy

The *hagirah* motif implies an unconditional commitment to and complete involvement with God at all times—from the initial stage of searching for God to the final stage of finding Him. In every phase, *homo absconditus*, hidden man, separates himself from his ancestral environment and becomes homeless, lonely, engaged in an almost incessant flight from his country and kindred. To meet God and confront infinity implies an act of transvaluation and heroic skepticism—a reappraisal of all goods and values, a shattering critique of all accepted categories and standards, a doubt concerning anything not directly related to this particular experience. The starting points for revelation and God-man communal existence are to be found in spiritual displacement, in brokenness, in the uprootedness of the human soul, in the disruption of human solidarities and flight from conditions pleasing and familiar. In order to behold God, one must go forth from his country and ancestral home.

Finding God engenders an existential crisis; *Adam revelatus*, revealed man, is supplanted by *Adam absconditus*. Suddenly, man is driven out of his natural community in which, until he discovered God, he felt quite comfortable. An indomitable force pushes him toward an unknown destination. To translate the ancient *hagirah* of Abraham into modern terms, I would say that the religious experience manifests itself in merciless criticism of all finite events, not excluding the most intimate relationships, such as those prevailing between a person and his next of kin (the natural community). A new world is born, and nothing is carried over to it from the old. Forsaking the most cherished friendships, the seeker follows the God whom he has met, by design or incidentally, into the unknown.

Disengagement, the main theme of prophecy, can be traced back to the very dawn of our history, to Abraham. Abraham had to go *mi-moladtekha*, "from your birthplace." The prophet must remove himself from his native environment. The environment into which we are born determines the way of our thinking, feeling, and striving. We think in terms of and via media with which we were confronted as a child. I still see my father and mother the way they looked when I was young, not the way they looked later in their old age. I have wandered from place to place, I have prayed in many synagogues, I have sat in many *sukkot*, I have celebrated many *seder* nights. However, when I visualize a Yom Kippur service, I see the *Beit ha-Midrash ha-Gadol* in Choslavitch, where I davened as a child, where I stood next to my father. When I reminisce, the environment of my childhood is reflected by those memories. To forget these pictures means to terminate one's identity. Memory is the very foundation of human identity, and if memory is cut off, the personality shrinks. And yet God told Abraham to forget.

The motif of abandoning the familiar and intimate because of a new and strange encounter is repeated in the episode of the *Akedah*. The Midrash (Gen. Rabbah 55:7) took note of the identical expressions in the first and last divine addresses to Abraham: "*Lekh lekha me-artzekha*" and "*Lekh lekha el Eretz Ha-Moriyah*." Which of these experiences was the more trying, the first or the last? Which was more heroic, to break with one's ancestral home and family, or to sacrifice one's son? Which ties were more meaningful to Abraham, the ties with his past or his future? The identical phrases express the same motif, the same idea; namely, that the person who finds God is homeless, fatherless, and childless—not biologically but spiritually. He is related neither to his parent nor to his child; he has to give up and disengage.

We find the same motif in the story of Elijah's first meeting with Elisha. When the prophetic call unexpectedly came to Elisha, this prosaic farmer forsook his farm and his parents; Instead, "He went after Elijah and he ministered to him" (I Kings 19:21). He became homeless and followed his new master into a mysterious, frightening world, into parts unknown to him.

A prophet is a wanderer, *na va-nad*, a nomad. He dwells wherever God wills him to abide. He must not be a man of property and rest. "And the Lord said to Abram, Go forth from your land, and from your birthplace, and from your father's house" (Gen. 12:1). Be always on the go, move continually from place to place, don't settle down. You have a task to fulfill, a message to put across. You must keep moving. Do not wait for people to come to you. In this verse, the Torah describes the destiny of the prophet.

Lekh lekha was the call of God to Abraham. Keep on journeying: You are but a wandering Aramean. You have no home, you have no country; you are dedicated to someone else. In order to become a believer, one must be the greatest, most outstanding non-believer; one has to go through the phase of not believing in time-honored principles and commonly accepted standards. Abraham, first of all, was a skeptic, doubting and questioning everything.

The disengagement motif receives expression in Maimonides' description of the prophet.

> When one abundantly endowed with these qualities of moral excellence, intellectual ability, and physical soundness enters *Pardes* [i.e., the experience of God achieved through certain types of inquiry] and continuously dwells upon those great and abstruse ideas and themes . . . sanctifying himself, withdrawing himself from the ways of the ordinary run of men who walk in the obscurities of the times, zealously training himself not to have a single thought of the vanities of the age and its intrigues but keeping his mind disengaged, concentrated on higher things as though bound beneath the celestial throne . . . (*Hilkhot Yesodei ha-Torah* 7:1).

I must emphasize that the religious personality's disengagement from and renunciation of the finite experience does not entail a monastic philosophy or an ascetic way of life. Judaism, as is well known, has enjoined man to share with God in the works of creation, to involve himself fully in the cosmic occurrence. What I intend to convey by using the terms "disengagement" and "flight" is that man, in spite of his physical and mental participation in natural events and processes, must never deal in absolutes with regard to finite creation, must never ascribe unlimited worth and supremacy to human achievements, institutions and values. He may cherish them, he may toil for their promotion, he may cultivate and guard them, he may enjoy them, and he may have pride in them. Yet he must not consider them as the *summum bonum*. Relativization of man-made values, ideals and institutions is a basic article in Judaism. The human creative mind deserves respect, attention, and appreciation, but it must never be made the object of adoration and worship. To believe that humanity is capable of solving all its problems alone, of bringing complete happiness and peace to the world, of arranging its affairs in an orderly fashion without soliciting divine aid and without accepting God's law, is contrary to the philosophy of disengagement.

If one places ultimate trust in his fellow men, then he has failed to fulfill the commandment of God, "Go forth from your land, and from your birthplace, and from your father's house." If one speaks in clichés, operates with meaningless categories that are in vogue, subscribes to public opinion about matters beyond the grasp of the average human mind, if one does not separate the wheat from the chaff in one's own mind and heart and with naive carelessness takes the common, the shallow, the empty phrase for granted, then one cannot be considered a straying wanderer. God wills man to probe, to explore the wide reaches of human existential experience, to deepen his self-awareness and world-awareness, and to discover for himself the incompleteness of our finite existence. In a word, religious criticism and skepticism render man a wanderer, homeless and displaced within the uncharted lanes of finitude.

The Estrangement of the Religious Leader

In light of the above, we may state that religious leadership demands of the individual whom God has elected the skill of skeptically appraising everything human along the entire spectrum of achievement, from technology to art.

The religious leader is a person who retreats from society into seclusion and loneliness. Again, this retreat is not physical but axiological. Abraham dwelt in a new world of values that were alien to his society. He dealt with the same facts as his contemporaries, but interpreted these primordial facts differently—not so much in an intellectual or scientific sense, but in terms of their meaning and value. The forms and figures into which his experiences were concentrated and objectified were not commensurate with the common mold. Between Abraham and his fellow men there was factual but not spiritual communication. In a word, the covenantal community's religious leader must be capable of being alone in his universe of values and ideals—not in the practical universe, but in the axiological universe. As Maimonides wrote,

> For it is known from statements made in Scripture that these four, namely the patriarchs and Moses, had their minds exclusively filled with the name of God, that is, with His knowledge and love. . . . When we therefore find them also engaged in commerce, in ruling others—in increasing their property and endeavoring to obtain possession of wealth and honor—we see in this fact a proof that when they were occupied in these things only their bodily limbs were at work, whilst their heart and mind never moved away from the name of God (*Guide* III:51).

Maimonides distinguishes between actual engagement in everyday activities and axiologico-spiritual withdrawal. Abraham worked for wealth, but this was not an absolute to him; it was not, so to say, his destiny. Something higher entranced him; something higher beckoned to him.

The leader must be ready and willing to tolerate abuse and humiliation. If he is spiritually homeless in the world of the mighty, a wandering Aramean among the complacent citizens of a proud and self-reliant society, he will be exposed to mockery. The outcry of the religious leader—indeed, of covenantal man— was echoed by the psalmist: "Have mercy upon us, O Lord, have mercy upon us, for we are exceedingly filled with contempt. Our soul is exceedingly filled with *ha-la'ag ha-sha'ananim*, the scorn of those who are at ease, and with the contempt of the proud" (Ps. 123:3–4)

La'ag is not so much scorn as ridicule or contempt. *La'ag ha-sha'ananim* refers to the smile and ridicule of those who are complacent, self-satisfied, proud. They have contempt for the person who brings restlessness into a community that wants to be at ease and comfortable. The stranger is always scoffed at; the lonely hermit is exposed to the ridicule of the vulgar, coarse, and stupid. People like uniformity; they resent the unknown and the unfamiliar, the immigrant and the newcomer. They even condemn the old-timer who tries to be different from the general run of the human mill, even if he does not differ in outward appearance, dress, language, or manners. They suspect him of cultivating some dream incommensurate with theirs. The crowd hates the individual who displays unique talents and hence departs from established patterns. Even in intellectual circles, people resent any departure from the beaten path in any field; the revolutionary scientist, the non-conforming artist, the social reformer are misunderstood and hurt by the scorn of critics. That is why Abraham the stranger, Abraham the wandering Aramean, was an object of mockery and derision. He was looked upon as a maverick, a peculiar sort of a person, a dreamer, a visionary, and particularly, more than anyone else, a troublemaker.

The episode narrated in the Bible about Abraham's departure from Canaan and his sojourn in Egypt (Gen. 12:10–20) is indicative of the lot of the poor wanderer. His beautiful wife was kidnapped—a traumatic, humiliating, shocking experience—and he was then deported from Egypt as if his presence posed a menace to the security of the country. Jeremiah stated: "For the word of the Lord was unto me a reproach and a mocking all day" (Jer. 20:8). A Jew entreats God thrice daily at the conclusion of his silent prayer: "And to those who curse me let my soul be dumb; let my soul be as dust to all." The Jew is a proud being who is aware of his mission and responsibilities. He does not enjoy abuse and ridicule. However, he knows that one who is spiritually different cannot escape humiliating situations, for his existential experience is incommensurate with the feelings and sentiments of others. Realizing one's destiny demands the ability to suffer disapproval and anguish at the hands of the crowd. Abraham emerged from this abysmal experience fortified and more determined than ever to climb to the upper reaches of his life.

Sarah called her son Yitzhak, saying, "*Kol ha-shome'a yitzahak li*" (Gen. 21:6). This can be understood to mean not that others will be joyful for me, but rather that "Whoever hears the news will laugh at and ridicule me." Why did God show Abraham and Sarah in an amusing, alas, even absurd, light that would provoke people to make scornful jests? Why did He at times present Abraham as a caricature that is subject to derision and banter?

The absurdity and laughability of Abraham's career reached its apex in the *Akedah* episode. Many are impressed by the tragic aspect of the *Akedah*, by the traumatic and dramatic experience of a heroic father about to lose his son. Abraham and Sarah had an experience that would have broken the body and shattered the spirit of anyone else. But this is not its greatness. God promised a son to Abraham, one who was supposed to perpetuate everything Abraham preached and everything he stood for. Years passed; Abraham and Sarah aged, their bodies weakened, and still they waited for the invisible God to realize His promise. Finally the impossible happened: Isaac was born.

Then the call came to Abraham to take his son, whose arrival he had expected patiently for so long, and sacrifice him. Did not people say that the relationship between Abraham and his God bordered on the insane and psychopathic? That Abraham worshipped a God of utter cruelty who rejoiced in the agony, misery, and anguish of His most devoted servants? That a God of viciousness and dreadful malice had somehow entranced Abraham and enslaved him? They laughed, they derided, they mocked and condemned him mercilessly. In the epic of the *Akedah*, the heroism demonstrated by Abraham expressed itself not so much in his readiness to incur martyrdom and the loss of a child as in his willingness to endure the scornful ridicule and derision of society. All this is a consequence of the new role foisted upon Abraham, that of the straying wanderer.

Abraham as a Social Being

There is another motif in Abraham, one that is just the opposite of the previous: Abraham as a social being longing for communication. Our lonely father was a loving man with a sincere affection for people. He was lonesome for companionship, the warmth and coziness of a life together. How could he be satisfied with his secluded life, with a hermit-like existence, with loneliness and continual withdrawal, when he was burdened with a great message which he had, willy-nilly, to deliver? He beheld a wonderful vision and was driven by an inner impulse to have others behold it. He wanted to build a new society and establish a new ethical order. All this cannot be accomplished by a hermit. The hermit can raise his own existence to great heights. He can dedicate himself to God and to God's service. But the great message cannot be delivered by someone who is continually engaged in a movement of recoil.

In order to realize his hopes and ideals, Abraham had to turn from repose to outer-directed activity, from retreat to forward movement. He could not have received God's message if he had not retreated from society. If he wanted to accomplish his mission and attain the objective, however, he would have to return to the society from which he had fled. The creative will in Abraham had to break through the barriers that separated him from society. Now he had to make his inner light visible to his fellow men.

Abraham was eager to step out of his private and intimate heritage into the public world of action and word. The hidden knowledge in Abraham was pressing for manifestation. The Abraham who at the outset had renounced his kin, deserted society, and intentionally displaced himself, who had chosen homelessness in preference to a together existence, now reversed his course and began to move in the opposite direction, toward society. He could no longer endure loneliness. He craved friendship, comradeship, and a communal life. In despair, he cried out to God, "Lord God, what will You give me, seeing I go *ariri*" (Gen. 15:2). *Ariri* does not only mean childless; it means lonely. Abraham did not cry out when God told him to move on from his ancestral home, from the land of his birth, to parts unknown, because he was engaged then in the movement of recoil, of withdrawal. He understood that in order to achieve, he must choose loneliness. But when the message ripened in Abraham, when the new world vision matured in him and the prophecy he had to deliver was pressing for manifestation, he understood that he could not accomplish this task in solitude; he had to return to society. When God told him, "Your reward will be great" (Gen. 15:1), he replied, What reward can I expect, how can I realize my mission, if I am alone?

Abraham wanted a child upon whom to pour out his love and affection. He wanted to love and be loved. He could no longer renounce his social will and the yearning for we-ness. He understood very well that friendship cannot grow out of surface communication and pragmatic associations, lovely as they may be. Friendship can be realized only in inner communion, in existential sharing, in creative relationships, in sympathy. Man cannot be redeemed from his loneliness through quick, childish camaraderie or casual and incidental acquaintanceships, but only through deep mutual understanding, a meeting of minds and hearts, and a feeling of togetherness that ties every thread of the personality into such a relationship. Such a communal existence is not possible when the individual has withdrawn spiritually from society. It is possible only when individuals, prompted by a common urge for creativity, join together in an undertaking that claims the whole of the person and that accords a true place to friendship.

Abraham therefore tried to create a community of the committed and dedicated, a covenantal community. He returned to the very people whose company he had rejected, whose friendship and concern he had refused to acknowledge, and tried to rediscover them, to affiliate with them, to find a common language with them, to communicate his great message to them. "Abraham converted the males, and Sarah the females" (Rashi, Gen. 12:5). Abraham, the straying wanderer, became a settler and a citizen—not of the old society, but of a new society, a very small one.

Abraham's fatherhood awareness was a distinct paradoxical experience that oscillated between two mutually exclusive poles, thesis and antithesis, complete repose and merger with others, withdrawal and forward-surging, aloneness and togetherness, exile and return. Abraham's biography begins with *"Lekh lekha"* and concludes, more or less, with "And he planted a grove in Beersheba" (Gen. 21:33). He planted a tree and he settled in Beersheba for many years. Finally settling down for good, Abraham gave up his nomadic life and became a citizen, a member of a community—the community he had created. At the twilight of his life, when the sun was setting, he understood he had somehow accomplished his mission.

Two wills were locked in a struggle: the will to move on, to flee, to wander, to forget, to renounce—and the will to stay, to strike roots, to form relationships, to create a fellowship, to share with a community the deepest secret of one's existential experience. There are two Abrahams, one the nomad who wanders with his sheep and the other, the builder of altars, the preacher of God's word, the signer of treaties, the citizen and comrade. "A stranger and a sojourner am I with you" (Gen. 23:4).

Out of this conflict of wills emerges a creative critical will characteristic of our historical role as a covenantal community of the committed. But while the will is creative, the gesture of creation is inseparably linked with negation and withdrawal. You cannot build unless you are ready to reject the old and obsolete. The creative genius must first free himself from his moorings to the established and accepted world into which he was born. Human beings are never born into a new society; they are born into an old society, and there is always something obsolete, something ludicrous, something foul in an old society. The creative genius takes his life in his own hands and rearranges it. He refuses to accept the ready-made, the completed, the prepared. He courageously defies fate, the insensate forces with which nature has surrounded him, and attempts to shape a new environment and a new community that will be guided by a great idea he has discovered that guides him like a lodestar. He defeats the existence foisted upon him by the meaningless order of facticity and creates new dimensions within which a free existential experience is possible.

The task of the Jew is to take fate (*goral*), and transform it into destiny (*yi'ud*). Abraham replaced an unalterable alien causal determination with meaningful inward decision. He acted upon his environment and changed it in accordance with a visionary blueprint he had discovered in his encounter with God. In a word, Abraham cast off his passive role as an onlooker witnessing the cosmic drama in all its glory and grandeur, and became a participant in this magnificent drama, an actor who intervenes in the work of creation. Abraham discovered, too, that God is an ethos and not simply a natural, cosmic deity interested solely in playing out a cosmic drama, like an engineer who wants to start a train moving. Abraham discovered that God and man are partners. God's mastery was replaced with partnership, a covenant by virtue of which two parties assume mutual obligations to each other. At this point, the covenantal community was born.

Of course, the juridic foundation upon which any contract rests is the idea of the equality of the two parties involved in the contractual commitments. Both parties possess inalienable rights which can be given away only by their mutual consent. Since the idea of the covenantal community has its origin in a juridic category, the contract, the experience of equality and freedom must be present in one's confrontation with God. There is, of course, an aspect of mastery, remoteness, and distance. However, when a member of the covenantal community encounters God, he encounters Him not only as a master, but also as a companion and friend. The whole idea of a covenantal community is nonsensical if God is experienced only in His transcendent majesty and remoteness, reigning supreme over creation, unapproachable, inexpressible, awe-inspiring, and daunting, one from whom man flees in fright and terror. The numinous encounter with God and covenantal association with Him are mutually exclusive experiences. The God of the covenant is not man's master but his friend. God is a leader and a guide, but at the same time a comrade and companion.

God said *"Lekh lekha"* and then joined the wandering Aramean on his journeys, roaming with him and showing him the land. "I took your father Abraham from the other side of the flood and led him throughout all the land of Canaan and multiplied his seed and gave him Isaac" (Joshua 24:3). God took Abraham by the hand, so to speak, and guided him on his journey through the land of Canaan. God and man, their hands joined in one firm grip, walked together in search of parts unknown, of a new community, of a new land, a new society, a new world. God likewise accompanied Jacob on his journeys. At Beth-El, while resting on the cold stones, Jacob suddenly realized that God was watching over him in a strange place and would accompany him wherever he went. "Behold, I am with you and will keep you in all the places where you go, and will bring you again into this land, for I will not leave you until I have done that of which I have spoken to you" (Gen. 28:15).

God moves with man from place to place, from home into exile, and, vice versa, from the alien land back to the house of his parents. God joined a shepherd community and Himself became a nomad. He escorted Jacob to Egypt. "I will go down with you into Egypt, and I will also surely bring you up again" (Gen. 46:4). It is for good reason that Jacob speaks of "the God before whom my fathers Abraham and Isaac did walk, the God who associated with me all my life unto this day" (Gen. 48:15). One can walk before God only on one condition—that God follows. Abraham and Isaac walked before God, and He moved on with them. God befriended Jacob and kept him company.

A very significant motif of our most intimate and personal religious experience finds expression in the idea of God walking with man—a theme later seized upon by Jewish mysticism and transformed into a great cosmogonic and theosophic mystery. Not only is Abraham a lonely, wandering being who cannot find shelter and refuge in a foreign world in which he finds it impossible to strike roots, but God, too, is a stranger in the universe He created. Both Abraham and God are homeless, searching for rootedness and permanency in this world of ours. God Himself lives in the works of His own creation as an exile, in retreat from society's ambitious and aggressive planning and vulgar doing. God and Abraham wander to faraway lands, suffering as shepherds and sojourners. *Shekhinta be-galuta*, the Divine Presence is in exile. Only the redemption of creation will free God from exile and isolation.

❧ Abraham the Teacher

God's Disillusionment

We cannot understand Abraham's educational mission unless we understand what preceded him: the sudden descent of creation from great heights into an abyss of corruption, evil, and sordidness.

The narrative in Genesis reveals to us a paradox. The Creator is disillusioned with His own creation! At twilight of the mysterious sixth day, when God cast a glance at the creation just born out of nihility, He said confidently that everything He had created was "very good, *tov me'od*" (Gen. 1:31). The world shone in its pristine beauty and purity. God was satisfied and content with His creation. If I may use anthropomorphic terms, He had a sense of fulfillment and accomplishment. Yet at the conclusion of the story of creation, the Bible tells us something that is simply shocking: "God saw that the wickedness of man was great in the earth, and that every imagination of the thoughts of his heart was only evil continually. And the Lord regretted that He had made man on the earth, and it grieved him at His heart" (Gen. 6:5–6). The world did not fulfill the Creator's hopes and will. It rebelled against its Maker, corrupted its creatureliness, and turned into a wicked affair. God regretted that He had created the world. He was disillusioned with his own works, disenchanted and disappointed. When God cast His glance at the world in Noah's day, He saw that it was not the world He had created. It had become corrupt and contaminated, abounding in moral evil and inconsiderateness.

What method did God employ to bring about a catharsis of the world, to purify it and purge it of evil? He punished all living creatures by exterminating them in the deluge. Living creatures serve man; if man is gone, there is no need for them. Noah then was charged with the same apostolic mission as was Abraham. The building of the ark is symbolic of the call issued to Noah, the summons to build and create a new society. Yet those who survived and came after this natural cataclysm did not improve; man was not redeemed. He remained as wicked as antediluvian man. Punishment, however severe, did not achieve the proper effect. Man still led a brute existence, and his intentions remained wicked. The idea of catharsis was not realized through the flood. It did not redeem man from sin and evil. God therefore decided that ruthless punishment would no longer be employed to purge creation of evil. "The Lord said in His heart, I will not again curse the ground anymore for man's sake; for the imagination of man's heart is evil from his youth; neither will I again smite any more every thing living, as I have done" (Gen. 8:21).

How, then, will man mend his ways? How will a new world be created? How will man become civilized and improve? Instantaneous and merciless intervention by God was ruled out as a method of influencing man's conduct, because the evil instinct is a part of the nature with which God endowed him at creation.

We then read, "While the earth remains, seedtime and harvest, and cold and heat, and summer and winter, and day and night shall not cease" (Gen. 8:22). What is the connection between the preceding verse about the evil nature of man and the unalterable, steady routine of nature? It is that just as there are no leaps or sudden transformations within the cosmic process, there are no leaps in human nature. A catastrophe, even of such enormous proportions as the deluge, cannot have a redeeming effect upon man, who is by his very nature wicked, a brute. That is where Christianity erred. Christianity thought in terms of an instantaneous, metaphysical, transcendental, supranatural redemption of man—not through destruction but somehow through sacrifice. Judaism does not believe in the spontaneous redemption of man.

The Educational Gesture

What is the alternative to instantaneous, redemptive catharsis on the part of a wrathful, jealous God? The answer, I believe, is to be found in the idea of the parent-teacher—in Abraham, the "father of many nations" (Gen. 17:5). In Judaism, "parent" means "educator," just as "disciples are called children" (*Sifri*, Deut. 34). Man may progress and grow if he is treated like a child whose talents, aptitudes, and moral qualities are gradually developed and sensitized by education. The Torah ruled out the possibility of a miraculous spiritual ascent by man through transcendental intervention and resigned itself to piecemeal elevation of the *homo sapiens*. An immanent process of education inspired by the parent-teacher is the way catharsis may be attained.

Man is entangled in wickedness; he is quite often guided by unclean and base instincts. Yet there is in him a great potential to attain the good and sublime. No human being, however deep his fall from God may be, has lost this divine endowment, the invisible and hidden treasure entrusted to him at creation—the image of God embedded in the most hidden recesses of his existential awareness. Therefore, no one, not even the most coarse and immoral individual, is immune to educational techniques and influences. We must not deny the possibility of redemption to anyone. Every heart, however tough and insensitive, can be softened; every soul, however sick, can be cured; every skeptic and agnostic can be touched if the educator knows how to touch the weak spot in his psyche—the vague yearning, the Ecclesiastes experience that all is vanity, the sense of an inner void. Every thick personality crust shielding one's tender feelings from being hurt may be infiltrated. Man was created with a capacity for growth and development—not in a natural sense, but spiritually—through education. He cannot "seize his powers in one act" (cf. Emil Brunner, *The Divine Imperative* [London, 1937], p. 504), but can through the cautious, meaningful, steadfast exercise of his mental aptitudes. This potential, the hyletic element in man, is present in everyone.

God, after the deluge, forsakes the idea of spontaneously and instantly redeeming man. He supplants spontaneity with a deliberate, well-planned, gradual educational gesture. This gesture is bound to succeed, for everyone can ascend the Mount of the Lord. It is only a question of speed and tempo. Man cannot be changed overnight; he must slowly learn to live in peace and justice with his fellow man. For this he needs a guide.

God was man's first teacher. God's role as a teacher was initiated after the deluge. God did not teach Adam; He simply gave him a command: "And the Lord God commanded the man" (Gen. 2:16). After the flood, God begins to reveal to man a moral code, the elements of a civilized social order. "But flesh with the life thereof, which is the blood thereof, you shall not eat. And surely your blood of your lives will I require; whoso sheds man's blood, by man shall his blood be shed, for in the image of God made He man" (Gen. 9:4–6). The mere fact that God begins to legislate a moral norm and teach man how to actualize it bears witness to God's trust in man's ability to fulfill the law and establish himself as a moral being. Otherwise, God's disclosure of the law would be a malicious mockery. Law cannot be given to man if he is incapable of actualizing it. The Torah has a deep understanding of human nature; if God gave man a moral code, apparently He thought that man still had a great potential for good despite his malicious, evil actions.

And God said: This is the token of the covenant which I make between Me and you—and every living creature that is with you for perpetual generations. I set My bow in the cloud, and it shall be a token of a covenant between Me and the earth. And it shall come to pass, when I bring a cloud over the earth, that the bow shall be seen in the cloud. And I will remember My covenant which is between Me and you . . . and the waters shall no more become a flood to destroy all flesh. And the bow shall be in the cloud, and I will look upon it that I remember the everlasting covenant that is between God and every living creature of all flesh (Gen. 9:12–16).

How does the rainbow symbolize the covenant between God and man that ensures humanity's survival on earth? The rainbow appears because of the refraction and reflection of the rays of the sun in the droplets of water contained in the clouds. I believe that the arc of multicolored light in the midst of a dark cloud symbolizes the luminous endowment of a lowly, obscure, absurd creature like man that reflects the supranatural light emanated by the Creator. God stands opposite man, even as the sun is opposite the cloud. He makes man susceptible to the educational gesture and guarantees his eventual rise from a brutish existence to a redeemed life. God does not want to exterminate mankind and all the other living creatures, because in spite of his remoteness from God, man is capable of redeeming himself through a slow ascent to the Almighty. The fate of the animals is intertwined with that of man. If man is able to rehabilitate himself, the animals too will be saved.

Man's salvation cannot be realized through supernatural intervention. The act of redemption is dependent upon the free will of man, exercised through his effort to develop the aptitudes and talents with which he has been blessed. If man could be redeemed by a supernatural act, his role would be passive and nil. Man would only be able to accept grace—as

Christianity says. However, salvation requires an educational process, and the teacher is not God alone. Man must cooperate with God to heal the broken essence of creation. Without man's aid, God will not restore the lost harmony of the world and pull man out of the abyss of depravity and vulgarity. Therefore God descended into the world of man and offered him a covenant that binds them within one existential community.

Adam did not understand the idea of the covenant. He rebelled against God and did not respond to His call of "*ayeka*, where are you?" (Gen. 3:9). Nor did Noah grasp the divine message about the covenant. Right after the story of the rainbow, Noah planted a vineyard, drank of the wine, became intoxicated, and was uncovered within his tent. The covenant was defiled. Noah's household was divided. The great vision of a united covenantal community faded. The selection of Noah was a failure.

Abraham was the first human with whom God formed a partnership. God prepared the blueprint for redemption; man was the engineer who put it into effect by actualizing his potential, drawing out of himself whatever was hidden in the recesses of his personality. This redemptive act is not spontaneous but piecemeal. It may take millennia to complete. Yet man should always behold the rainbow in the dark cloud, the great divine light in the darkness of the existential night of human fall and corruption.

"When Abram was ninety-nine years old, the Lord appeared to Abram and said unto him, I am the Almighty God; walk before Me and be perfect" (Gen. 17:1). I am the omnipotent God who created the universe, who governs the cosmos and watches over it lest creation slip into the abyss of nihility. Yet in spite of My unlimited power over natural causal processes, I need your help in perfecting and ennobling man. Divine force—My primordial will embedded in inorganic and living matter, which makes stones fall, the tides rise and recede, the flowers blossom, and the human organism function—cannot redeem man and elevate him to a higher existence. The great, endless cosmic force at which everyone marvels cannot redeem man. Only a concerted effort by man and God can shape a new human personality and save mankind from a meaningless, brutish existence. Walk before Me, and we will both wander from place to place teaching people, educating them and implanting in them the seed of a new faith and a new ethos. Walk before Me, and your perfection will be attained through a joint endeavor of man and God, of finitude and infinity, yours and Mine. The catharsis of man is linked with the act of teaching. Abraham, walking with God, became the pedagogue *par excellence.*

The covenantal teacher is given the superhuman task of joining God in the noblest of works, the perfection of man. Abraham is cognizant of what the task involves: a summons to a life which, on the one hand, is lonely and strange, inner-directed, removed from society and normal camaraderie, committed fully to the God-experience—an all-consuming, all-absorbing love that requires withdrawal from everything else; but which, on the other hand, is also dedicated to the creation of a new society, to one's fellow man with whom one desires to form a covenantal community including the I, you, and He.

The religious teacher is always on the go, wandering, searching, exploring. God's voice drives him to move on constantly lest he be seduced by the enticing beauty and splendor of an idolatrous world. He is restless, full of despair about man and his doings, yet burning with a great love, a passion abounding in hope. He is the optimist *par excellence.* Elijah was a perfect incarnation of the wandering Aramean. He walked through the bustling capital city of Samaria, which was teeming with luxury, abundance, and wantonness; but he walked as a stranger, mysterious and detached, negating the worth of the goods to which his contemporaries were committed, preaching the law of God and portending His wrath. No one knew where he came from or who his parents were. He was a wanderer, a stranger, a solitary being always on the run, who finally disappeared in a storm and vanished from human sight into the great, awesome beyond.

Yet the religious leader is also a builder of society, a sociable man who yearns for friends and companions. He is a teacher and educator who has indomitable faith in human potential, in man's ability to do what ought to be done instead of just letting things happen at random. Abraham severs social bonds and yet is capable of forming much stronger inter-human relationships, social commitments, of giving of himself unreservedly to society. He is critical but not pessimistic; he reproaches without condemning; he is disturbed but not desperate. He transvaluates all values and standards. Yet one great value he retains: the inner worth and unlimited capacity of man, to whose moral promotion and perfection he dedicates his life.

At this point Abraham emerges as—to use a Kierkegaardian term—the Knight of Faith. "And he believed, *he'emin,* in the Lord, and He counted it to him as righteousness" (Gen. 15:6). *He'emin* is the *hif'il* form of the verb *a-m-n*, which signifies raising, bringing up, educating: "And he brought up (*omen*) Hadassah, that is, Esther" (Esther 2:7); "They that were brought up (*ha-emunim*) in scarlet embraced dunghills" (Lam. 4:5); "Then I was by Him as one brought up (*amon*) with Him, and I was daily His delight" (Prov. 8:30).

The *hif'il* form denotes a causative element, either with regard to the other (in the sense that I cause others to engage in a particular action) or concerning oneself (if the action requires a special effort; see, e.g., Rashi, Ex. 14:10). To believe, to have faith, to bring up, and to raise differ only as to their grammatical forms. To believe implies a causative element, an endeavor by the doer to perform the act.

Judaism apparently considers the act of education to be synonymous with the act of faith. Indeed, educational endeavors require of the teacher patience and the ability to wait for results; to work ceaselessly without obtaining immediate and tangible benefits; to invest energy, time, and attention without being rewarded the next instant; to turn one's face to the future and sacrifice continually for a great vision that may never be realized during the teacher's lifespan.

It is not implausible to link the verb *a-m-n* to *em*, "mother," since she is the foremost teacher of and believer in the child. A mother will never despair of her child, nor will she spare any effort to further her child's welfare, even though she does not expect to live long enough to enjoy the fruits of her toil and sacrifice. She is the most unselfish being. Her faith in her child can never be shaken. She will patiently try to do some particular thing for her child over and over again, since failure, however disappointing, does not weaken her determination to bring out the best and finest in the child. The *em* is unconditionally committed to her child, in whose capabilities she has unrestricted trust.

To believe and to bring up are identical accomplishments. The believer must be able to engage in a great educational task, to pick up the debris of a shattered world and reconstitute a harmonious creation, to seize human talent and capability in an ongoing array of deeds, suffusing these powers with meaning and integrating them into a redeemed personality. The believer is committed to the reconstruction of human society and the catharsis of the individual. All this must happen in a natural, evolutionary way, through progressive action, while man, like an infant, learns to take his first ascending steps up the steep mountain of the Lord.

The element of faith is indispensable for any pedagogical endeavor. A teacher who lacks confidence that his pupil is able to grasp the ideas he passes on to him will never be successful. The teacher must also have faith that learning will have a moral impact upon the disciple. We believe that knowledge is redemptive and therapeutic performance. A pessimist must never do any teaching or be entrusted with the care of a child, since his efforts are doomed to failure from the very outset. All educational activities are identical with mothering, for what is mothering if not displaying unlimited faith in a child?

Abraham had such faith. The proof is his intercession on behalf of Sodom. Abraham asked that God not destroy Sodom and its satellite cities if there be ten righteous people in each city. *Prima facie*, we do not understand Abraham's request. Why shouldn't the Almighty punish the wicked and save the righteous? Why did Abraham intercede with God that no harm be done to the entire city? Where is the logic?

Abraham believed that the righteous would, in the course of years, change the whole structure of the city; the righteous would succeed in bringing the wicked back to God. Abraham held the view that a teacher is all-powerful and that there is nothing he cannot do. That is why he said, "Shall not the Judge of all the earth do justly?" (Gen. 18:25). There is hope for every human being, including the most wicked. Abraham exhibited limitless patience and, disregarding the injustice and vulgarity with which he was treated from time to time, continued to preach the name of God. Noah lacked this kind of faith, and therefore failed as a teacher.

In a word, the religious leader is an instructor, a teacher, an educator charged with the mission of completing God's works; he is the helper and companion of God through a dedicated effort of gradually enlightening the ignorant, ennobling the vulgar and coarse, revealing to man his great capability and leading him toward a great destiny. He must have faith in God and, at the same time, faith in man; he is both a *ma'amin* and an *omen*, patient and courageous. Abraham was such a person.

The Will to Teach

Education is the actualization of a potential hidden in the child. To educate means to discover, to open up, to develop and draw out. The youth is a bundle of possibilities, unformed and indefinite. It is the job of the educator or parent to mold a personality out of the human hyle. The child is taught not only how to exercise his innate capabilities, but also how to grow and achieve something above and beyond his natural capabilities; not only how to find himself, but how to find others as well. In a word, the child should be taught how to transcend himself, how to rise above and beyond his latent powers and capabilities.

This paradoxical idea is rooted in the concept of free will. Maimonides said that everyone can be righteous like Moses (*Hilkhot Teshuvah* 5:2). How can we fulfill the aspiration to be like Moses? Such greatness is surely not granted to everyone. The answer is obvious. Judaism believes that we can achieve more than our potential. We are capable of climbing to heights greater than what nature has assigned us. There are two capacities in man—one psychological and the other metaphysical. Man summons the whole of his being, not only his body and mind but the very existential center of his personality, the mysterious and transcendent personality that abides in the shadows. This metaphysical personality is bestowed upon man by his teacher. Education is not simply supervision of the child during his years of maturing, but active participation in his progress. A disciple is a merger of two personae. The teacher gives the student a part of himself, and an existential union is formed.

Every prophet was a teacher. The prophetic *kerygma* was addressed to the community, to the many. The Halakhah states that a prophet who suppresses the message given to him commits a grave sin (*Hilkhot Yesodei ha-Torah* 9:3). A prophecy always commences with the imperative: "Hear, I beg you; Give ear; Thus says the Lord; Go and say; Prophesy." The very term *navi*, prophet, is derived from *niv sefatayim*—meaning "speech," literally "fruit of the lips" (Isa. 57:19).

With Abraham, the situation was different. At the outset, Abraham received no specific instructions to deliver a definitive message since he alone, without help from a transcendental or human source, discovered the truth. It was *his* truth, *his* message, which he attained through his own work and untiring efforts. The Almighty wanted Abraham to find Him naturally, rationally, gradually. He also willed Abraham to teach in a spontaneous, free fashion without being coerced by a transcendental vision. At the very outset, Abraham taught the fruits of his painstaking effort, his sleepless nights and searching days.

Why did Abraham teach? He was not commanded to do so. Rather, he was motivated by two things: an inner will to teach and kindness, *hesed*. The will to teach is an aboriginal urge. Teaching means overflowing, spilling over into another mind. A person who knows little will hardly experience the desire to communicate whatever he knows to others. Only if and when you are filled to capacity with knowledge does it begin to spread beyond the limits. In a word, teaching means the flow of excess knowledge from one individual to another. In this context, teaching is not effort or action; it is a spontaneous process. A person overfilled with knowledge unburdens himself by teaching and passing on the knowledge to another. Through teaching, one releases intellectual pressure. It is the gratification of a pressing need.

Maimonides writes in the *Guide of the Perplexed* (II, 37):

> But he may also receive such a prophecy as would compel him to address his fellow men, teach them, and benefit them through his perfection. It is clear that without this second degree, no books would have been written, nor would any prophet have persuaded others to know the truth. . . The characteristic of the intellect is that he who receives an additional degree of the influence is compelled to address his fellow men under all circumstances, whether he is listened to or not, even if he injures himself thereby. Thus we find prophets who did not leave off speaking to the people until they were slain.

It is the divine influence that moves them, that does not allow them to rest in any way even though they bring great evils upon themselves. When Jeremiah was despised, he decided to withhold his prophecy, but could not. "For the word of the Lord was unto me a reproach and a mocking all day, and I said, I will not preach, nor will I again speak in His name; but it was in my heart as a burning fire enclosed in my bones, and I was wearied to keep it and did not prevail" (Jer. 20:8–9).

Abraham preached, rebuked, debated, and mainly taught because he could not act otherwise. He taught compulsively, like Jeremiah hundreds of years later.

While the urge to teach is personalistic and metaphysical, there is also another urge, one that is of a moral character: teaching as an act of *hesed* or *caritas*. *Hesed* consists of an existential communal awareness, an open and not closed life, a life not as a castle or fortress but as an accessible tent. "He sat at the entrance of his tent in the heat of the day" (Gen. 18:1), sharing a common existence instead of holding everything for himself.

The principle of *hesed* mandates providing not only material but also spiritual goods. The Bible decrees, "If your brother waxes poor and his means fail with you, then you shall uphold him; as a stranger and a sojourner shall he live with you" (Lev. 25:35). This law is related not only to economic poverty but also to spiritual deprivation. Just as we are duty bound to feed the poor and clothe the destitute, we are equally obligated to teach the ignorant, dispel prejudice and superstition, and enlighten those who live in darkness. To teach is an act of great charity.

As a matter of fact, Abraham combined the two kinds of *hesed*, material and spiritual: "He planted a grove in Beersheba and called there in the name of the Lord, the God of the world" (Gen. 21:33). Rashi cites two Talmudic interpretations of the "grove," both of which relate to Abraham's hospitality: either the grove was to be a source of fruit for his guests, or he built an inn for wayfarers (*Sotah* 10a). At this grove, Abraham also engaged in a dual educational act: he preached "the name of the Lord" and he also taught the name of "the God of the world." In order to understand the distinction between these, let us look at two doctrines with which Maimonides commenced his *Sefer ha-Madda*.

First, "The foundation of all foundations and pillar of all wisdom is to know that there is a First Being who brought all existing things into being; all beings in heaven as well as earth exist only through His true existence" (*Hilkhot Yesodei ha-Torah* 1:1). This article of faith is to be found in the sentence "He called there in the name of the Lord." *Havayah*, "the Lord," represents faith in God as the existence *par excellence*. This is more than an article of faith; it also means to experience God everywhere. Maimonides then adds: "This being is the God of the world and the master of nature, and He is the prime mover of the spheres . . ." (*ibid.* 1:2). In other words, it is not enough to believe in God at an ontological and metaphysical level by being aware of our existential roots or origins. If God is the mover of the universe and is present in nature, if God sustains creation, then He is also concerned with human behavior and wills man to follow in His steps and act morally. Faith in God precipitates new moral norms. God is not only transcendental and numinous, but also "God of the world," supervising and guiding us together with the boundless cosmos, concerned with every detail within the universe.

In his descriptive portrayal of Abraham, Maimonides similarly writes that Abraham discovered a double truth: "He realized that there was one God," and also that He "controlled the sphere and had created everything" (*Hilkhot Avodat Kokhavim* 1:3). Abraham's discovery of God had both metaphysical and ethical meaning. When he started to spread his doctrine, he began with "the name of the Lord," and as he progressed he also taught them "the God of the world." Abraham would teach while practicing hospitality, for that was of the essence of his teaching.

Abraham intended to convert mankind, the whole world, to monotheism and the morality of *hesed*. "Then he began to call in a loud voice to all people, informing them that the entire universe has but one Creator and it is proper to serve Him; he went from city to city and from kingdom to kingdom, calling and gathering together the inhabitants until he arrived in the land of Canaan" (*Hilkhot Avodat Kokhavim* 1:3).

Abraham's journey apparently took a long time. He finally arrived in Canaan, but later had to leave it: "There was a famine in the land, and Abram went down to Egypt *lagur sham*, to sojourn there" (Gen. 12:10). We remember the quotation about Jacob from the Haggadah: "*Lagur sham* indicates that he did not go down to settle, but only to stay [temporarily]. As it is said: 'And [Joseph's brothers] said to Pharaoh, We have come *lagur sham*, to sojourn in the land' (Gen. 47:4)." Abraham left the Land of Israel temporarily, intending to return when the famine would pass. Perhaps his sojourn there would be a long one. But *lagur* also implies to retain one's identity, to carry on a mission, to remain loyal to a great vision. That is why Rashi (Gen. 32:5) says with regard to Jacob that there is an equation between *Im Lavan garti* ("I have sojourned with Laban") and *taryag mitzvot shamarti* ("I have observed the 613 commandments"). I served Laban for twenty years, says Jacob, but I retained my identity. I did not give up an iota of Abraham's tradition.

We then read, "As he was about to come, *hikriv lavo*, to Egypt" (Gen. 12:11). There is another place where the Torah uses the *hif'il* form of this word, *hikriv*, instead of the *kal* form, *karav*. When Pharaoh was pursuing the Jews, the verse says "*u-Phar'oh hikriv*" (Ex. 14:10) instead of "*u- Phar'oh karav*." As Rashi (ad loc.) points out, *hikriv* means that he made a special effort to arrive as soon as possible. According to Rashi, the intransitive *karav* may be replaced by the corresponding *hif'il* form in order to amplify the action. Pharaoh was so excited about bringing the Jews back to Egypt and putting them to work at their former tasks that he made a special effort to catch up with them as quickly as possible. That is also why the verse in Genesis uses *hikriv*. Here, too, Abraham had to make a special effort, because he wanted to stay in *Eretz Yisrael*. He had to compel himself to leave the land. Pharaoh struggled to speed up his army. Abraham fought against himself.

However, in my opinion, it is also true that Egypt attracted Abraham. He knew that if he succeeded in persuading Pharaoh that polytheism and idolatry were wrong and that there is one God who wills man to lead a moral life, then the battle between paganism and monotheism would be won. Egypt was the metropolis of the Middle East, the seat of a developed technology and civilization. Her influence was powerful. If Egypt were to join Abraham, the redemption of mankind would be achieved quickly. Abraham had not succeeded in persuading the people of Chaldea, the second cultural center of antiquity. Nevertheless, he tried again in Egypt—only to fail there, too. Even so, the disappointing experience in Egypt did not discourage him from pursuing his original goal—the total redemption and conversion of mankind. "And he went on his journeys from the Negev to Beth-El, to the place of the altar which he had made there at the first; and there Abram called on the name of the Lord" (Gen. 13:3–4).

In short, even though he failed completely in his undertaking in Egypt, Abraham clung tenaciously to his ideal; he did not give up his commitment. He returned to the site where he had built the altar before his journey to Egypt and there he called on the name of God. The universal ideal was Abraham's lodestar. Persecution, ridicule, indifference, opposition, loneliness—none of these experiences discouraged him. He was persistent and determined.

Kedushah and Tzedakah u-Mishpat

Abraham sought to achieve two objectives: *tzedakah u-mishpat* ("righteousness and justice") and *kedushah* (holiness). God says, "I have known him, that he may command his children and his household after him, that they may keep the way of the Lord, *la'asot tzedakah u-mishpat*, to do righteousness and justice" (Gen. 18:19). In my opinion, the translation of *la'asot* as an infinitive, "to do," is questionable. The verse should be rendered: "that they may keep the way of the Lord *and they may do* [instead of 'to do'] righteousness and justice." (Similar grammatical constructs can be found in the verses "which God created *la'asot*, and made" [Gen. 2:3] and "For on this day He shall forgive you *letaher etkhem*, and purify you" [Lev. 16:30].) In other words, Abraham's testament was twofold: keeping the way of the Lord, which requires *kedushah,* and also practicing righteousness and justice.

Wherever Abraham attempted to teach, to inform, and to enlighten, "there he built an altar" (Gen. 12:7). An altar, of course, is synonymous with sacrifice. This principle was central both in Abraham's universal activities propagating the morality of justice and charity and in his covenantal undertaking emphasizing *kedushah*, the way of the Lord. The difference between the universal altar and the covenantal altar expresses itself in the number of sacrifices brought upon them. In comparison with the covenantal sacrificial activities, the claims of the universal altar are very modest and few in number. From a halakhic viewpoint, the universal mission of Abraham crystallized in seven *mitzvot*, the covenantal mission in 613.

It is commonplace to say that the ideal of *tzedakah u-mishpat* is related to relations between man and his fellow man, *bein adam le-havero*, while the term *kedushah* refers to the specific relationship between God and man, *bein adam la-Makom*. This is erroneous. The norm of *kedushah* is all-inclusive. It embraces the total structure of human activity. In fact, when the Torah speaks of being holy and enumerates the areas where one is called upon to exercise *kedushah*, most of them are *bein adam le-havero*. Indeed, the altar upon which one has to sacrifice his own selfish interests in order to realize the demand for *kedushah* is much larger than the altar built by the person concerned only with *tzedakah u-mishpat*.

Let me cite a well-known example (brought by Rashi, *Makkot* 24a, and Rashbam, *Bava Batra* 88a, with its source in *She'iltot* 36). Rav Safra offered a diamond for sale. A gentile aristocrat made an offer for the diamond, but Rav Safra was reading the *Shema* and could not accept the offer, even though he was perfectly satisfied with it. The prospective buyer, thinking the lack of a response meant that Rav Safra had rejected his offer, increased it. Rav Safra, who was not through with *Keri'at Shema,* still did not reply. The buyer increased the offer again. In the meantime, Rav Safra finished the *Shema*; he turned to the buyer and said that he would sell him the stone at the price of his first offer because he had decided to do so when the offer was made.

Hazal say that Rav Safra was a *dover emet bi-levavo*, truthful at heart (*Bava Batra* 88a, *Makkot* 24a). Analyzing the story from the standpoint of *tzedakah u-mishpat*, it is quite obvious that Rav Safra would not have violated the norm of truth even if he had sold the stone for the highest bid, since to be truthful at the level of *tzedakah u-mishpat* concerns only commitments made to one's fellow man. Had Rav Safra said, "I accept the first offer," or had he at least responded to the bid with a nod of his head, then reneging on the original promise would have been a violation. However, there was no deal here between vendor and purchaser. Rav Safra simply thought to himself that he would sell the diamond for the initial offer. Why should the thought bind him? The answer is plain. From the standpoint of *kedushah*, one must be truthful not only to others but even to oneself.

Let me share a more recent example. A story is told about Reb Yoshe Ber of Brisk that one *erev Shavu'ot*, late in the afternoon on his way to the synagogue, he noticed a flower stand that was still open. He went over to the woman and said: "My dear, it is late. We will usher in the *Yom Tov* pretty soon. Why don't you go home to your family?" "Yes, Rabbi," the woman answered, "but I haven't sold any flowers. The count sent in a wagon loaded with flowers, and everyone brought greenery from the count. In fact, his flowers and branches were much better than mine. What shall I do, Rabbi? There is nothing in the house, no food, no wine, no candles! I have nothing to look forward to."

Reb Yoshe Ber told the woman to step aside. He took her place and began to announce aloud how beautiful the flowers were, how tender and green the twigs and leaves. People suddenly encountered a strange scene. Their world-renowned rabbi in his festival garments was zealously selling flowers—and charging exorbitant prices. Of course, all the flowers were sold quickly despite the prohibitive prices.

Whether the story is true or untrue, the fact that such a folk-story is told is indicative of the demands the Jew makes upon his own conscience as regards *kedushah*. In other words, to help someone in distress, you must sacrifice not only your money but your very dignity and pride. This conception is the product not of the idea of *tzedakah,* but of *kedushah*. To help others is not only an ethical act but also a great experience through which you come one or two steps closer to the Almighty. Serving one's fellow man is *eo ipso* the most sublime service to God.

On the other hand, *mitzvot bein adam la-Makom* can also represent the idea of *tzedakah u-mishpat*. A person who fulfills his duties to the Almighty complies not only with the idea of *kedushah* but with that of *tzedakah u-mishpat*. One must exercise righteousness and justice in relationship to God.

The world belongs to God. He is its master and rightful owner. Our status here is that of a tenant permitted by the owner to live on his property. Indeed, man does not own even himself. Whatever he has—talents, capacities, instincts, feelings, thoughts, intuitive flashes—belongs to the Almighty, Who in His grace told man to share in His world. The contractual arrangements are conditional, however, and subject to annulment in case of a violation of the rules of the tenancy. Hence any sin renders man a thief or a robber. He forfeits his rights because he did not live up to the terms upon which he and God both agreed. Consequently, in violating *mitzvot she-bein adam la-Makom* man *ipso facto* acts contrary to the principle of righteousness or justice, since he usurps rights he lost by sinning. He steals from God. "Will a man rob God? Yet you rob Me! But you say: Wherein have we robbed You? . . . You are cursed with the curses, yet you rob Me" (Malachi 3:8, 9). To sin, to not give tithes to the poor, or to violate any other precept is equal to robbing or misappropriating God's property. To comply with all the precepts means to practice righteousness in one's relationship to God.

One can even practice charity with regard to God; here we come across a mystery. I remember that I once asked my rebbe a question when I was probably six or seven years old. It was in the early autumn, a few days or a week before Rosh Ha-Shanah. The rebbe was in an excellent mood. He had permitted us to take our desks out into the orchard, and in the shade of apple trees laden with ripe fruit, he explained to us the idea of *Malkhuyot*. He simply translated *"Al ken nekaveh lekha."*

He told us that the Almighty waits for mankind to appear and kneel before Him, recognize His kingdom and kingship, and give Him the crown. This great event of coronation will occur at some point in the future; we do not know when and how. However, we know with absolute certitude that it will happen. Then the whole world will find its redemption. Evil will vanish, death will be banished, and the tears wiped off the countenance of every man. Every Rosh Ha-Shanah we engage in a rehearsal of that great dramatic event, the coronation of God. We Jews recognize His kingship and majesty now, and we wait impatiently for the universal coronation to take place.

"Rebbe," I asked, "God is the creator and maker of everything. He sustains the world. Should He turn away His countenance, everything would crumble into chaos. He is all powerful and all-knowing. If God is eager to redeem the world and to be proclaimed King of the universe, then why does He have to burden His people with the task of enlightening the people and teaching them the way of the Lord? Why do we have to wait thousands of years for the universal redemption? Why does man have to hand the royal crown over to Him instead of Him taking the crown all by Himself and placing it upon His head? Why does man have to consent to God's universal kingship?"

The rebbe gave an answer which I did not understand well at the time. Later, when I grew up and had some insight into Jewish thought, I realized that there is a great hidden mystery of *Melekh asur ba-rehatim*, the captive King: "Your head upon you is like the Carmel, and the hair of your head like purple: the king is held captive in the tresses thereof" (Song of Songs 7:6).

True, God is the source, the origin of being; nothing exists besides Him. All worlds, the visible and the hidden, share in His infinite existence. He is omnipotent. His will reigns supreme throughout the charted and uncharted spaces of the universe. Not a single pebble can violate the law He has embedded in matter. As regards the revelation of God through the cosmic drama, man's role is zero. However, as for the revelation through general and Jewish history, God surrendered, so to speak, His power to humanity in general and especially to the members of the covenantal community. He is the King who holds Himself captive.

He willed the Shulammite to play an active part in the redemption process of humanity. She, not God, has the initiative. He turned it over to her. The king is held captive! The *Shekhinah* waits for Israel to redeem Her. It is a mystery! God does not proclaim His kingship; He waits for everyone to accept His kingdom.

God the Almighty wills man, the helpless and weak being, to march ahead of Him. He wants man to seize the initiative and plot the course of events; then the Almighty will complete it. By acting in this manner, man—so to speak—exercises charity with regard to God.

In a word, both sets of categories—*tzedakah u-mishpat,* on the one hand, and *kedushah,* on the other hand—are universal. Both systems of commandments—*bein adam la-Makom* and *bein adam le-havero*—pursue the dual goals of *kedushah* and *tzedakah u-mishpat.*

God placed a double load upon Abraham's shoulders: a universal one and a covenantal-private one. Abraham's task consisted in teaching the world as well as in teaching his son, enlightening tens of thousands of people and at the same time instructing a single individual and gradually forming a covenantal community that seeks God. The second task Abraham fulfilled successfully; a covenantal community was formed. Abraham also succeeded in civilizing and enlightening his household, which encompassed tens of thousands. However, it was not required of them to share the destiny of those who accepted the covenant. That is why only seventy souls descended from Canaan to Egypt.

The covenantal community's job is to teach—again, not by word but by deed. In fact, there were not two commitments on the part of Abraham. There was one commitment: to enlighten mankind and to bring about its redemption through the acceptance of God's kingdom. Yet, in order to teach, one must adopt an exalted lifestyle, practicing *kedushah* at the highest level. For even the most insensitive and cruel will be defeated by *kedushah*. Its fascination is invincible. Its power is irresistible.

"It came to pass that night that the angel of the Lord went forth and smote in the camp of the Assyrians a hundred fourscore and five thousand, and when men arose early in the morning, behold, they were all dead corpses" (II Kings 19:35). The Talmud (Sanhedrin 95b) tells us, "R. Isaac the smith said: He unsealed their ears for them, so that they heard the celestial beings sing [praises to God] and they died, as it is written (Isa. 36:3), 'At Your exaltation the people were scattered' ".

The satraps of Sennacherib, vulgar, cruel and insensitive, were confronted suddenly with a great song of *kedushah*. Their ears were opened to a sweet, breathtaking, and irresistible melody. They heard a music the likes of which they never heard, and it aroused in them a strange drive, an incontestable urge to change their lives into something different. The longing was so strong that their souls, in their flight toward the spaces from which the melody was flowing, departed their coarse and blood-stained bodies.

It takes a long time to bring mankind back to God. But no matter how slow the process, Abraham will finally emerge victorious, and everyone will bow to God.

❧ Partnerships
Fulfilled and Frayed

Sarah

"Abram went up from Egypt" (Gen. 13:1). Of course, travel from Egypt to the Negev is physically an upward movement, climbing a hill. But we can also interpret the verse in a metaphoric fashion. After his experience in Egypt, Abraham rose to new heights. His sojourn in Egypt somehow enriched his personality, opening up new vistas for him. When he returned to *Eretz Yisrael*, he was not the same Abraham who had left; he returned with more imagination and a bolder, more aggressive outlook on the world. Abraham's experience taught him how long a way it was that he—and perhaps not he alone but countless generations after him—would have to travel before his ideals would be realized and achieved. Egypt was the center of material civilization, the technologically and industrially most highly developed, well-organized state. We still admire the Egyptians for their pyramids, their astronomical and mathematical knowledge. However, basic principles of morality were alien to them. Abraham was ready now to be patient and to wait, to work, and not to despair. Abraham came back to *Eretz*

Yisrael a different Abraham, more imaginative, more experienced, more sensitive.

When Abraham originally set out for Canaan, we are told, "Abram took Sarai his wife" (Gen. 12:5). When Abraham left Egypt, the verse should have said "he and his wife Sarai," but instead it says only "he and his wife" (Gen. 13:1). Whenever God addressed Abraham about Sarah, He never said "your wife" but "your wife Sarah." When Abraham arrived in Egypt, we read "he said to his wife Sarai" (Gen. 12:11), but two verses on it says that "the Egyptians saw the woman" (Gen. 12:14), an anonymous woman. Her name is intentionally left out. Then, "The princes of Pharaoh also saw her, and praised her to Pharaoh; and the woman was taken into Pharaoh's house" (Gen. 12:15). Again her name is omitted! But when God acts to protect her, Pharaoh and his house were smitten with plagues *"al devar Sarai*, because of Sarai, wife of Abram" (Gen. 12:17). Not one verse in which God addresses Abraham about Sarah fails to include Sarah's name. But "Pharaoh commanded his men concerning him; and they sent him away, and his wife" (Gen. 12:20). She has no name; "And Abram went up from Egypt, he, and his wife, and all that he had" (Gen. 13:1). The Torah is bent upon emphasizing that the very instant he crossed the border into Egypt, Sarah lost her name and suddenly became a wife with no name. Yet when the Torah speaks about Abraham leaving Haran and departing for Canaan, she is "Sarai the wife of Abram."

The name Sarai means "princess," a very important woman. Sarah's status in the history of Judaism is not only that of being Abraham's wife. After all, he had more than one wife, but Keturah and Hagar—whether they were one person or two different women—have not been immortalized and perpetuated in Jewish history. No, the fact that Sarah was married to Abraham was not enough to give her a permanent place in the Jewish historical household. Rather, Sarah in her own right was a major figure, as important as Abraham—as a matter of fact, *Hazal* say she was *superior* to him (Ex. Rabbah 1:1). When Sarah gave him the order "Cast out this slave and her son," the Torah says that "the thing was very grievous in Abraham's sight because of his son," but God instructed him: "Let it not be grievous in your sight because of the lad and because of your slave; in all that Sarah has said to you, listen to her voice" (Gen. 21:10–12). Abraham would not have succeeded without Sarah's coopera-tion; all his efforts would have been in vain had Sarah not stood by him.

But Sarah was a prominent person, superior to Abraham, only as long as they were in Canaan. From the very moment they crossed the border into Egypt, no one cared about Sarah, about her spiritual personality, her leadership, her talents and capabilities, her status as a prophetess. "The Egyptians saw the woman, that she was very beautiful." The Egyptians looked at women only from one perspective—whether they were physical-ly attractive. Therefore they were punished *al devar Sarai*—because they degraded Sarai, a great and singular person, by regarding her merely as a comely, anonymous woman.

That was the difference between the community of Abraham and the Egyptian community. Abraham looked upon his wife as *Sarai,* "my ruler." Abraham never told her what to do; on the contrary, she told him what to do. She was not only beautiful; she was a spiritual figure on par with Abraham. "God said to Abraham, 'As for Sarai your wife, you shall not call her name Sarai, but Sarah shall her name be; and I will bless her. . .' " (Gen. 17:15–16). When God says that He will bless her, He blesses not with money or material riches, but with ability, with charisma, with spiritual endowment. Sarah will be superior to all other women. "She shall be nations; kings of peoples shall be of her" (Gen. 17:16).

The very instant Abram's name was changed to Abraham, the symbol of power and mastery was added to Sarai's name, the *heh* replaced the *yud*. When God addressed Himself to Abraham about his own name, He said, I am changing the name

Abram to Abraham: "No longer shall your name be called Abram, but Abraham shall be your name" (Gen. 17:5). But when He addressed Himself to Abraham concerning Sarah's name, He said: "As for Sarai your wife, you shall not call her name Sarai, for Sarah is her name" (Gen. 17:15). Do not call her Sarai, because her name is already Sarah; God informed Abraham that her name was already changed. When was it changed? When Abraham's name was changed. Abraham cannot be *av hamon goyim*, the father of many peoples, if Sarah is not simultaneously crowned as the mother of those peoples. There was an existential interdependence between Abraham and Sarah.

In a word, at creation man and woman together, and only together, achieved human dignity, *imago Dei*; similarly, when Abraham and Sarah were elected by the Almighty, they, too, achieved, and again only together, covenantal sanctity.

Lot

At the beginning of *Lekh Lekha,* we read: "Abram went forth as the Lord had commanded him, and Lot went with him (*ito*)" (Gen. 12:4). Then we read: "Abram took Sarai his wife, and Lot his brother's son, and all their possessions that they had gathered, and the souls that they had made in Haran" (Gen. 12:5). Why the redundancy?

In fact, there is no real repetition. Abraham prepared to leave "as the Lord had commanded." The command was "*Lekh lekha* . . . from your father's house." Abraham apparently understood *lekha* to mean *levddekha*, "by yourself." Do not take anyone except your wife and the community of converts you have created. Do not try to persuade Lot to follow you. Abraham was determined to leave Haran the way God had told him to, and that meant leaving Lot behind. But Lot went with him, most probably responding as Ruth said to Naomi, "Your people shall be my people, and your God my God; where you die, I shall die, there I shall be buried" (Ruth 1:16–17). Lot became a member of Abraham's household; there was no difference between his wife Sarai and Lot. Abraham apparently adopted the son of his brother Haran. He raised Lot, reared him, educated him. He was his son.

However, when the Torah begins to tell us about Abraham's departure from Egypt, we read "Abram went up from Egypt, he and his wife" (Gen. 13:1); Lot is no longer a member of Abraham's family. Something happened in Egypt. Lot somehow separated himself from Abraham and his family. *"Ve-Lot imo"*— Lot also traveled with him, but no longer as a member of Abraham's family. *Imo* signifies two equals. When Lot set out with Abraham from Haran, we are told *"va-yelekh ito Lot"* (Gen. 12:4). When something is part of a bigger thing, *et* is used. When Abraham moved from Haran, Lot merely accompanied him, *ito.* He did not feel an equal of Abraham; he understood that Abraham was head and shoulders above him. It was not so easy to dislocate and wander with Abraham, to find a land whose name he did not know. But apparently Lot was completely loyal to Abraham; he believed in him and had confidence in him. He went *ito,* not *imo*; he followed him, he did not travel with him. But after Egypt there was a change in Lot, *"ve-Lot imo."*

The Torah explains: "Abram was very rich in cattle, in silver, and in gold" (Gen. 13:2); "and Lot, *ha-holekh et Avram,*" who all his life was a follower of Abram, "had flocks, herds, and tents" (Gen. 13:5). Lot was also very rich, as rich as Abraham; he thought he was just as important as Abraham. Abraham had reared Lot and certainly tried to implant his *Weltanschauung* in him. In Egypt, Abraham discovered that his work with Lot was in vain. Rashi (Gen. 13:5) tells us that Lot, too, was heavily laden with gold and silver because of *halikhato im Avram*—he was a partner of Abraham. Abraham managed his estate so well that Lot too accumulated great wealth. All of Lot's worldly success was due to the fact that he was a member of Abraham's clan, but Lot disregarded that. How many times has a father built a business and accumulated wealth, and then his son begins to rebel against the old man and finally drives him out of the business?

Abraham was disillusioned with Lot. Sarah was a barren woman. Who if not Lot, he thought, would take over the spiritual empire he was trying to build; who would propagate his philosophy? Then, suddenly, Abraham realized that he had made a bitter mistake. Lot was spiritually not his son. Biologically, of course, he was his kinsman, "*anashim ahim anahnu*" (Gen. 13:8). A link of blood is a very strong bond and Abraham could never sever it; but it was by no means a spiritual bond.

Abraham lost his disciple, his *talmid*, in Egypt. If you know anything about *Hazal's Weltanschauung*, you know that they considered losing a *talmid* catastrophic, a disaster of mountainous proportions. Rabbi Yohanan lost ten of his children, but this tragic experience did not break him. He used to carry in his pocket a small bone of his tenth son to show the bereaved whenever he had to pay a condolence visit (*Berakhot* 5b). When he lost his *talmid* Reish Lakish, however, his grief was so great that he lost his mind. The Rabbis prayed for him to die as quickly as possible because for the great Rabbi Yohanan such a life was degrading (*Bava Metzia* 84a). The loss of ten children could not break him, but the loss of one *talmid* did.

The Gemara (*Berakhot* 17b) tells us that when the Sages would conclude their studies and take leave of the *beit ha-midrash* of Rav Hisda for the day, they would offer a prayer, "May there be no breach, and no going forth, and no outcry in our streets" (Ps. 144:14): May we not have an experience like the one Saul had with his disciple Doeg the Edomite; may we not encounter the bitter experience of Elisha, who lost the disciple Gehazi. Elisha did not lose Gehazi physically, he lost him spiritually; the same is true of Doeg. Abraham had to live through the same horrible experience.

We should not think that all this happened in just a few days—that Abraham arrived in Egypt, a day later Sarah was kidnapped and brought into Pharaoh's palatial home, the following day Pharaoh gave a deportation order, and finally, the very next day, Abraham was deported. Because the verses follow each other and the events in *Humash* unfold with great speed, we form the incorrect impression that everything happened in a few days. But Abraham might have been in Egypt for years—who knows how long! Egypt was the world's most advanced country, and Abraham was a shepherd. Lot was completely overpowered and overwhelmed by the stupendous Egyptian culture, civilization, and technology. He could not resist the influence of the environment. Abraham could, Sarah could, but Lot couldn't. Here is the acid test of a Jew: can he resist environmental pressures, can he withstand the impact of a culture that is materially great but morally and ethically very primitive?

Why did God cause a famine to develop in the land, forcing Abraham to go to Egypt? Rashi (Gen. 12:10) says that the purpose was *lenassoto*—to test his faith, to test how Abraham would react to Egyptian culture and civilization, to an entirely new environment. Would he be overwhelmed and succumb to Egyptian society, to its ideals, its philosophy, its views? Or would Abraham resist and emerge triumphant? God then repeated the test twice more—with Jacob in Haran and with Joseph in Egypt—to show that a Jew can live in exile and still retain his spiritual identity, either in poverty and in need, as a day-laborer or shepherd, or in riches and luxury as the prime minister of a foreign country. The Torah tested the patriarchs because the tests of the patriarchs were characteristic and indicative of the destiny of their descendants. That was the main purpose of bringing Abraham to Egypt.

There is a second reason why Abraham sojourned in Egypt, one that I know from my own experience. When one lives with parents, it is impossible for a son or daughter to not be critical of them from time to time. "For there is not a just man upon earth, that does good, and does not sin" (Eccl. 7:20). The child picks up on such things, some inconsistencies. In my youth, I occasionally harbored critical feelings toward my father and even toward my grandfather. Most everyone has at some time gone through this rebellious state against parental authority. When did I realize that the life of my father, my mother, my grandfather was a beautiful life, a moral life, and a dedicated and meaningful life? It was when I went to Germany. I did not live among Nazis; I lived in an intellectual community in Germany, and I saw gentiles who were considered moral. However, when I began to compare them with my grandfather and my father, I found that there was no comparison. We must wander through many foreign lands and experience numerous alien cultures. We must meet the greats of these nations and their intellectual and cultural giants. Only then will we revise our approach to our own forebears. We must observe the lifestyles of the leaders of secular culture in order to truly appreciate the greatness of the halakhic masters and the glory of our ancestral tradition.

In Berlin, I spoke with Yaakov Gromer, an associate of Albert Einstein. He was also once a *talmid* of my grandfather, Rav Hayyim Brisker. But he left Brisk and went on to become a great mathematician. He was not observant, but many a time you used to find him with a Gemara. He had an excellent head and could "learn." He told me, "When I was in Brisk, I found many faults with Rav Hayyim, but when I came to Berlin I realized that Rav Hayyim was a saint. They told me Einstein was considered a moral person, and he was indeed a moral person. But Rav Hayyim had more kindness"—he used the word *hesed*—"in his little finger than Albert Einstein had in all his heart and brain." One cannot understand the beauty of Judaism without encountering people of another culture. That is why Abraham had to go to Egypt—to see what Egypt was. It was fascinating at that time, and very attractive. Perhaps Abraham sometimes wondered whether life wasn't better in this wonderful, powerful, respected, rich state. Nevertheless, he came out of Egypt not only retaining his identity, but also spiritually more powerful. He grew to great heights. Adversity and opposition made him appreciate his own worldview all the more. But Lot succumbed.

After leaving Egypt, Abraham went on his journeys, *"va-yelekh le-massa'av"* (Gen. 13:3). The plain meaning is that Abraham did not travel continuously, but made many stops on the journey from Egypt to Beth-El. Rashi (Gen. 13:3) tells us that "he used to stop at the same inns in which he stayed on his way to Egypt." This, he says, teaches a rule of courtesy: If one has the habit of stopping over at a certain inn, one should not change (*Arakhin* 16b). When Abraham went to Egypt, he was a poor man materially. When he left Egypt he was very wealthy. If a man becomes rich and is now a prominent and respected member of society, it should not influence his habits and associations. He should not drop old friends in favor of new aristocrats—this is not the way of Abraham. On his way to Egypt, Abraham had to stay in cheap inns. Now he could afford better. But he did not change his habits or betray friends.

Another explanation for his stopping off at the same lodging houses where he stayed on his way to Egypt, says Rashi, was to repay his debts. He borrowed money on the way to Egypt because he was poor. The people trusted him. On the way back, he paid back his debts. The fact that he never deserted a friend, poor or rich, sinner or saint, is important. But is it important to tell us that he repaid a debt? Not paying a debt is prohibited by the Torah: "You shall not defraud your neighbor" (Lev. 19:13). But Abraham was now a millionaire; he owed only a few dollars to this one or that. He could have sent the money by messenger. However, he himself had borrowed the money, so he paid it back himself. He went to the house, and in addition to the payment, he thanked them. *Mitzvah bo yoter mi-be-sheluho* (*Kiddushin* 41a)—even though one can appoint a plenipotentiary to do a mitzvah on one's behalf, ideally one should do it personally.

The Torah says: "Abram was very rich in cattle, in silver, and in gold" (Gen. 13:2). Lot's riches are described as "flocks, herds, and tents" (Gen. 13:5). There is no mention of tents in connection with Abraham. The shepherds lived in tents and Lot had many shepherds; that is why he had so many tents. Abraham surely also had many shepherds, but Abraham was modest and did not display his wealth. Lot was ostentatious, wanting people to see his material success and respect him for it.

Both Abraham and Lot were rich, "and the land was not able to bear them, that they might live together" (Gen. 13:6). There was not enough pasture for them, not enough feed, so a quarrel developed. No feud, let alone one between people of higher caliber like Abraham and Lot, is precipitated by a shortage of pastureland. If Abraham and Lot wanted, they could have resolved this problem easily without creating a schism. After all, they had money, and they could have bought more pastureland; surely there was enough land for sale. But the trouble was that Abraham and Lot could not dwell together *spiritually*. Abraham and Lot did not have their old mutual respect and appreciation. There was no harmony between them.

They could not live *yahdav*, "together." The word *yahdav* refers to a merger of interests, common commitments, two people joining together and living by one ideal, one dream. They suffer together, rejoice together, sharing good moments and bad moments. This harmony between teacher and pupil, between uncle and nephew, which had been so perfect before, was somehow affected in Egypt. Lot now had different ideas and different dreams; there was no commensurability between their world views. Of course, when people become alienated intellectually, the estrangement finds its expression emotionally. Love turns into antagonism, sometimes into hate, resentment, and protest.

The Torah tells us how the tension began. "There was controversy, *riv*, between the herdsmen of Abram's cattle and the herdsmen of Lot's cattle" (Gen. 13:7). Interestingly, "Abram said to Lot, Let there be no strife, *merivah,* I beg you, between me and you, and between my herdsmen and your herdsmen, for we are brothers" (Gen. 13:8). There is a difference between *riv* and *merivah*. *Riv* means an argument: "If there is a controversy (*riv*) between men" (Deut. 25:1). This does not mean that the people hate or resent each other; even two friends can litigate. *Merivah*, however, means hatred, resentment, complete alienation. The shepherds had nothing to quarrel about; it was an argument that reflected the disharmonious relationship between their masters. They felt that something had changed between Abraham and Lot; their old harmonious relationship, their old deep-seated friendship, had changed. If the masters quarrel, the shepherds quarrel, too.

Abraham understood very well that if they continued to dwell together and to journey together, then finally they would become enemies. If two people do not like each other, if there is antagonism and tension between them, the best policy is to separate and get away from each other. Interestingly, Rashi comments on the verse "If you will take the left hand, then I will go to the right; or if you depart to the right hand, then I will go to the left" (Gen. 13:9) that "Wherever you will settle, I will not be too far away; I will be for you a shield and a helper." Even though I suggest separation, says Abraham, I promise that whenever you face adversaries, whenever you are in a crisis, I will come to your aid. I do not want this schism which is *beini u-veinekha*, "between me and you," to come out into the open where everyone will know about it. Civilized, spiritual people can hide their feelings as long as they are merely antagonistic to each other. They do not have to display their dislike and resentment publicly. But if the shepherds have already noticed the tension between you and me and are starting to quarrel—*u-vein ro'ai u-vein ro'ekha*, "and between my herdsmen and your herdsmen"—then everyone in Canaan will know that Abraham and Lot are at loggerheads, and it is a house divided against itself. That is why the Torah prefaces Abraham's words to Lot with the information that "the Canaanite and the Perizzite lived then in the land" (Gen. 13:7). If the feud comes out in the open, I will have to debate you in the open; we will be locked in an ideological struggle. I will preach righteousness and justice, and you will preach something else. I will preach faith in one God, and you will preach idolatry. I will lose all the sentiments and emotions I have for you. If we want to save some of what I feel for you as an *ah le-tzarah*, a brother in time of need—even though you are no longer my *ah le-de'ah*, a brother of like mind—let us separate immediately, "for we are brothers."

According to Rashi, the phrase "and the Canaanite and the Perizzite lived then in the land" (Gen. 13:7) indicates something else. Lot's shepherds used to let their cattle graze in the pastureland of other peoples. Their excuse was that the land belonged to Abraham anyway, Lot was his obvious heir, and thus the land would ultimately belong to Lot. But the Torah says "and the Canaanite and the Perizzite lived *then* in the land" (Gen. 13:7). In other words, the land did not yet belong to Abraham. Furthermore, the Torah says "*To your seed* will I give this land" (Gen. 12:7), not to you. The promise of the land pertained to Abraham's children. The dispute between Lot's shepherds and Abraham's was not about pastureland; it was about the principle of stealing, of *hamas*. The Torah, according to Rashi, describes the alienation of Lot from Abraham as having progressed so far that Lot no longer cared about the first and most important prohibition in Abraham's code, the one against stealing. Interestingly, this involved theft from foreigners, from enemies, but that does not matter. Halakhah also prohibits theft from gentiles. Whether the gentile is my friend or my enemy, stealing is prohibited. The prohibition of theft was one of Abraham's guiding principles, and Lot did not observe it. That is why Rashi interpreted the *riv* to be not about pasture but about principle, about *gezel*.

"And Lot lifted up his eyes, and saw the valley of the Jordan, that it was well watered everywhere, before the Lord destroyed Sodom and Gomorrah, like the garden of the Lord, like the land of Egypt, as you come to Zoar. Then Lot chose for himself the valley of the Jordan; and Lot journeyed east, and they separated themselves, one from the other" (Gen. 13:10–11). Later, Abraham too lifted up his eyes. "Then on the third day Abraham lifted up his eyes" (Gen. 22:4), and he saw the place to which he was going, Mount Moriah. That is what attracted Abraham's attention. Lot raised his eyes to see pastureland—that was all he wanted to see, nothing else. Of what else could Lot dream? Could he dream of God, of Mount Moriah, of eternity?

"Then Lot chose (*va-yivhar*) for himself the valley of the Jordan." *Behirah* means giving priority to one thing over another when there are two options. Lot indeed had two alternatives. He could have answered Abraham, "Let's forget what happened; now I want to join you again in your adventure." But "Lot lifted up his eyes, and saw the valley of the Jordan." He was charmed by it; he was overwhelmed. In his perception, "it was well watered everywhere . . . like the garden of the Lord" (Gen. 13:10). To his imagination, to his boundless fantasy, it meant more money, more cattle, more tents.

Lot understood Abraham's greatness, but he simply did not want to follow in Abraham's footsteps. He understood that Abraham's life was a dedicated one, that it entailed hardships and sacrifices. He loved Abraham, but in Sodom he saw another way of life: a comfortable life without sacrifice, without preaching, without building, and without revolutionizing society. Finally, he made his decision.

🐝 The War Between
the Kings

Caught in the Middle

The Torah is not interested in Abraham as an individual. Private episodes with no direct relevance to the unfolding of the great drama of Jewish existence are omitted. Abraham's story is important insofar as he is the father of the nation; I believe that the story of Abraham's going to war symbolizes our eternal destiny.

The Torah speaks here about two military blocs, two alliances. Likewise, Ezekiel described the war of Gog and Magog, the famous war that will precede the arrival of the messianic age. There mankind is divided into two great military, political, and social blocs. Gog is the northern one, Magog the southern—and the Jew is caught between them. To take another example, in the first Jewish commonwealth, disaster came because there was a great conflict between Egypt and Babylonia. And while Jeremiah warned against it, the Judean kingdom cast its lot with the wrong partner, Egypt. We were involuntarily caught in the clash of two world powers.

In Abraham's time, one bloc consisted of Amraphel king of

Shinar, who, according to *Hazal* (*Eruvin* 53a), was Nimrod. "Kush fathered Nimrod, he was the first on earth to be a mighty one" (Gen. 10:8). He was a victorious warrior, "a mighty hunter before the Lord" (Gen. 10:9). He expanded his territory: "The beginning of his kingdom was Babel . . . in the land of Shinar; out of that land went forth Assyria, and built Nineveh, and the city Rehoboth, and Calah" (Gen. 10:11). Like every great emperor and conqueror, he built new cities and thereby helped advance material civilization and technology.

Nimrod "*himrid et kol ha-olam kullo,* led the entire world to rebel against [God's] kingship" (*Eruvin* 53a). According to *Hazal*, the generation of the dispersion was intoxicated with its own material success and technology. "Let us build us a city and a tower with its top in the heavens" (Gen. 11:4). Let us dethrone the Creator. Man reigns supreme and, by applying his mind, can conquer the universe. The generation of the dispersion sought power. *Hazal* say that if a worker fell to his death, they didn't care; but if they lost a brick, they would mourn for it (*Pirkei de-Rabbi Eliezer* 24). They were power-loving, power-crazed, power-intoxicated. Abraham rejected the generation of the dispersion (*Avodah Zarah* 19a). He saw a generation that had gone berserk and was mad for power.

Opposing this bloc, there was another, represented by Sodom, which had "dust of gold" (Job 28:6). Its inhabitants were very rich and lived in luxury. This bloc represented the human quest for unlimited pleasure. Thus there was a clash of two powers, two military alliances, two armies. But more than that, there was a clash of two outlooks on the world, of two "ethical" systems, so to speak. The pleasure-seeking bloc, the representatives of the generation of the flood, served Chedorlaomer twelve years, "and in the thirteenth year they rebelled" (Gen. 14:4).

Chedorlaomer and the kings who were with him made a tremendous march on the eastern side of the Jordan River. The Torah projects a very strange picture. Chedorlaomer and his allies wanted to attack Sodom, Gomorrah, Admah, Zeboiim, and Bela because they were the rebels. But on the way to conquer them, they attacked the entire population of the eastern valley (Gen. 14:5-7). There was no clemency; wherever they went, they smote the population and conquered the territory. Then "the king of Sodom went out, as did the king of Gomorrah, the king of Admah, the king of Zeboiim, and the king of Bela, which is Zoar, and they waged war against them in the valley of Siddim; against Chedorlaomer the king of Elam, and with Tidal king of Goiim, and Amraphel king of Shinar, and Arioch king of Ellasar; four kings against five" (Gen. 14:8-9).

The Torah repeats "four kings with five." Sodom and Gomorrah, Admah, Zeboiim, and Bela had very fertile land. Their army was larger. And yet the four defeated the five, the fewer defeated the stronger, because they were better warriors (Rashi, Gen. 14:9). They were disciplined; they represented an ideology of power and dominion, a life dedicated to an ideal. But the five were softened by voluptuousness and the quest for lust. They were not trained or disciplined, and therefore they lost.

Of course, both blocs were opposed by Abraham. He would have wanted to remain neutral, outside the entire drama of the clash between these two mutually exclusive ideologies and political systems. Suddenly, Abraham was pulled in, for Lot was taken captive. At this point, Abraham had to side with one bloc against another; he had no choice. We cannot imagine Abraham as an ally of Sodom and Gomorrah, of people who were "exceedingly wicked and sinners before the Lord" (Gen. 13:13). But he couldn't help it, as Lot was a prisoner.

Why was Lot taken captive? He did not have to pay tribute to the four kings; he did not rebel against them. But he was Abraham's nephew. Somehow Chedorlaomer decided that Lot was responsible for the rebellion. If not for Lot, he said, Sodom and Gomorrah would have remained loyal and subservient; they would still be vassals, and I would not have these problems. When Chedorlaomer needed a scapegoat, he did not blame the king of Sodom. He chose Lot. Abraham and Lot had "separated themselves, one from the other" (Gen. 13:11), not only geographically but also ideologically. When Lot settled in Sodom, he embraced its people and their ideas. As a matter of fact, on the day the angels came to him he had just been appointed a judge over them (Rashi, Gen. 19:1). His patriotism and his complete surrender to their philosophy were not questioned. Lot was completely integrated in their society, but it did not help him.

When Jews are accused of crimes they never committed, the assimilated Jew who is estranged from his people and thinks that he is completely integrated into the non-Jewish community is still regarded as Jewish. Assimilation does not protect a Jew from sharing in Jewish destiny. "They took Lot, Abram's brother's son, who lived in Sodom, and his goods, and departed" (Gen. 14:12), even though he was a full-fledged, complete Sodomite. This story is relevant because it is telling us not about one single event, but about a recurring feature of Jewish history.

During his march, Chedorlaomer smote the Refaim, even though they were "great and many, and tall, like the Anakim" (Deut. 2:21). Apparently the Refaim could do nothing against Chedorlaomer, who, with his allies, led a powerful, crushing war machine. The Refaim succumbed and were immediately exterminated, but one of them escaped. *Hazal* say it was Og king of Bashan (*Niddah* 61a). Og managed to flee, and he brought Abraham the message "that his brother was taken captive" (Gen. 14:14).

Hazal suggest that Og brought Abraham the news that his nephew had been taken prisoner because he hoped that Abraham would be killed and he could then marry Sarah (Gen. Rabbah 42:8). But I believe that Og had another motive. Og had the intuition of a non-Jew that whatever physical power could not accomplish, Abraham—with his determination, spiritual leadership, devotion, and dedication—would accomplish.

Abraham had not trained his people to fight with weapons but with the spirit and readiness to sacrifice. Thus Abraham might prevail—as did the Jews in Israel in 1967.

When Abraham heard that Lot was taken captive, a normal reaction would have been, "It serves him right; I warned him not to cast his lot with the Sodomites." Lot had rejected Abraham and his demanding God (Rashi, Gen. 13:11), preferring a pleasure-seeking society to Abraham's covenantal fellowship. Yet Abraham did not react this way: "And when Abram heard that *his brother* was taken captive . . ." (Gen. 14:14). A Jew must feel a duty to save his brother even if his brother has departed from the righteous path. Loyalty is the first mark of Abraham.

In fact, Lot remained his brother not only biologically, but even spiritually. The great faith of a Jew is that no matter how alienated his fellow Jew is, there is within him some potential, some spark that can be built into a great flame. We have no right to give up on any Jew. "Even though he has sinned, he is a Jew" (*Sanhedrin* 44a).

Abraham is called here *Avram ha-Ivri* (Gen. 14:13). He stands "on one side," *me-ever ehad,* and the entire rest of the world on the other (Gen. Rabbah 42:8). "Abram the *Ivri*" means Abram the singular one, the lonely one, Abram from the other side of the river. The story of Lot cast light upon Abraham's destiny. No matter how hard a Jew may try to erase his Jewish identity, no matter how integrated and assimilated he is, no matter how remote he is from the great heritage which Abraham tried to hand down to him, no matter how patriotic he is, and no matter how great his contribution is to the general community or society—he still remains an *Ivri*. In the same verse, we learn that Abraham "lived in the plains of Mamre the Amorite, kinsman of Eshkol and Aner, these were confederate with Abram." But when "the one who escaped" came and told him that Lot had been taken prisoner, Abraham understood how useless was his covenant with them, that the covenant was good only as long as it served the interests of Mamre and Eshkol and Aner. According to the midrash cited by Rashi (Gen. 14:24), they did not join him in the battle to recover Lot, but merely stayed behind to guard his belongings. Suddenly Abraham became aware of the loneliness of the Jew.

The episode of the warring kings teaches us many things. First, the Jew is caught in the titanic struggle between two powerful blocs in world history. A Jew can never be an outsider to great events; he is always entangled, against his will, in great events that take place. Second, even though Abraham rejected both ideologies—the ideology of pleasure and the ideology of power—he had to side with one of them, because the other had captured Lot. Third, when caught in the whirlwind of history, the Jew is carried like a leaf in the dark autumnal night; there is no difference between a loyal Jew and an assimilated Jew, between Abraham and Lot. On the contrary, Lot was more exposed to danger. Fourth, Abraham must understand that his destiny is one of loneliness. Such is the unfolding of the great drama of Jewish existence.

Melchizedek's Blessing

When the Torah relates the story of the encounter between the king of Sodom and Abraham, it begins, "And the king of Sodom went out to meet him" (Gen. 14:17). Then it suddenly interrupts the account of the meeting between the king and Abraham and tells us about another meeting, the one between Melchizedek and Abraham. The king of Sodom was the one Abraham had saved. He had lost his throne, his people, his state—everything. Certainly he was supposed to greet Abraham the way Melchizedek did, extending a welcome to him, and bringing out bread and wine, food for the famished and weary warriors. But the king of Sodom came out for a different reason, to ensure that whatever Abraham had rescued and saved should be turned over to him. Of course, he started out in a nice diplomatic way: "Give me the persons, and take the goods for yourself" (Gen.

14:21). But he really wanted the goods too, not only the persons.

Melchizedek came out with bread and wine to feed the warriors. He was a disinterested party, an outsider, an onlooker who had witnessed the struggle between Abraham and Chedorlaomer. Melchizedek was not indebted to Abraham, but he was decent and fair; he understood what Abraham had accomplished and he came out to greet him. Rashi (Gen. 14:18) says that this was the way decent people would greet warriors who were famished from battle, weary, tired, and exhausted. Abraham and his victorious army had crossed *Eretz Yisrael* from the north and passed Jerusalem. In antiquity it would have taken weeks to get to Jerusalem from Damascus. No doubt their movement was slow; they could not race along if they had to take care of cattle, women, children, and all the prisoners. We know what a victorious army does, even now in modern times. In antiquity, a famished victorious army on a march back from the battlefront, intoxicated with victory, saw nothing as sacred. Robbery, rape, murder, licentiousness, gluttony—all these were permissible. But Abraham's army was different. Coming back after weeks of fighting and moving through the land, they were still famished and starved. On the way, there were many settlements, cities and villages, from which they could have gotten food if they had wanted, but no one had touched anything.

"Melchizedek king of Salem brought forth bread and wine; and he was the priest of the Most High God. And he blessed him, and said, Blessed be Abram to the Most High God, possessor of heaven and earth" (Gen. 14:18–19). We would have expected Abraham to be blessed *by* God, *me-E-l Elyon*. But Melchizedek uses the dative: blessed *to* God, *le-E-l Elyon*. This means that Abraham's blessing had to reflect back upon God. His blessing had to be useful, so to speak, to the Master of the Universe. God bestows blessing upon man, but the blessing is reflected back to God. Melchizedek's blessing was that Abraham would succeed in his service of God, in his great undertaking, his great commitment, his great endeavor to establish a new society and give man a new code by which to live and act. May all the blessings God bestowed upon Abraham be returned with dividends to God. May Abraham proclaim that God owns the world, that He is the master of the world, and that man is only an instrument in the hands of God to carry out and to realize the Almighty's will.

Melchizedek continues: "*U-varukh E-l Elyon*, and blessed be the Most High God, who has delivered your enemies into your hands" (Gen. 14:20). The order should have been reversed. First he should have recited praise to God, who had delivered all enemies into Abraham's hands, and then he should have blessed Abraham. Why did he change the order?

How can a human being, a tragic, fragile, helpless being, praise the Almighty, the Eternal One who created the cosmos? A human being cannot give anything to God, nor can he detract anything from God. We say, "*Barukh attah,* Blessed"—not praised—"are You, our God, the King of the universe." But if He is the King of the universe, how can we address blessings to Him? How can a lowly creature address blessings to the Eternal and Infinite One, to the *Ein Sof*? Isn't it a *contradictio in objecto*?

The answer is that God is blessed if people rise to the great opportunity God has offered them. God can be blessed only if man achieves great heights, if man leads an ethical and saintly life, if he is obedient and constructive, if he does not misuse his intellectual ability for destructive purposes. Only then will the Kingdom of God be expanded to embrace the whole universe. God is exalted when His people achieve a high level of exaltedness, when human beings realize the full potential with which God has endowed them, when they become active and creative on behalf of God, when they realize the image of God that grants them spiritual personality. The Almighty is somehow dependent upon man, for it is through man's endeavor, adventure, determination, and commitment that God's name becomes exalted. This is exactly what we mean when we say *Barukh attah*. We should be worthy of serving God; we should understand the great opportunity He offers us and we should be capable of rising to the occasion and attaining great heights.

Therefore, Melchizedek could not start by saying *Barukh E-l Elyon*, because without Abraham God could not be blessed. One Abraham is enough to make a blessing possible and reasonable. So before he blessed God, he had to bless Abraham to be successful—successful not in accumulating riches for himself but in carrying the banner of his new philosophy, his new code, his new way of life. *Barukh Avram le-E-l Elyon*—let Abraham be successful in his dedication, in his determination to serve God, in his commitment to God. Melchizedek understood very well that the blessing had not yet been realized in full. Abraham must conquer the world spiritually; the whole world would have to join Abraham in praising God, in walking in His ways, in attaining the highest good. Let Abraham be fully successful, let him emerge triumphant from his engagement with a cynical, immoral, and at times stupid world, just as he emerged victorious from his physical engagement with Chedorlaomer. If Abraham is successful, then God will be blessed, because the blessedness of God can only be realized by having man actually serve Him.

We do not know who Melchizedek was. Rashi (14:18) quotes a midrash that he was Shem the son of Noah (*Nedarim* 32b, Targum Pseudo-Yonatan). We see that when Abraham came with his new philosophy of monotheism, there were other individuals who also knew about it. Melchizedek was the king of justice. "He was the priest of the Most High God" (Gen. 14:18), a servant of the Almighty. His philosophy was identical with that of Abraham. He was a contemporary of Abraham and apparently accepted the same certitudes, the same articles of faith, the same moral norms Abraham had formulated. Why didn't he join Abraham? Together they would have been much stronger. Not long before, the Torah had called him *Avram ha-Ivri*, lonesome Abraham, lonely Abraham: "The whole world on one side, and he on the opposite side." Where was Melchizedek? Apparently, he was so overwhelmed by Abraham's victory that he had to give expression to his amazement. Abraham had defeated all the kings! But after this episode, Melchizedek disappears. We heard nothing of him before and we will not hear of him after. That is the difference between Abraham and Melchizedek. Whatever Abraham knew, whatever Abraham treasured and considered precious and worthwhile, he wanted to share with others.

Abraham later says to the king of Sodom, "I have lifted up my hand to the Lord, the Most High God, the Possessor of heaven and earth" (Gen. 14:22). Interestingly, the phrase *"E-l Elyon Koneh shamayim va-aretz"* was coined not by Abraham but by Melchizedek! And this phrase was incorporated in our *Amidah* prayer. Melchizedek had beautiful ideas, but he was never able to implement them. Abraham's greatness consisted not only in inventing ideas, in coining beautiful phrases, but in taking ideas and converting them into reality, into facts.

❧ An Eternal Covenant

A New Drama

"After these events, the word of the Lord came to Abram in a vision" (Gen. 15:1). The phrase *ahar ha-devarim ha-eleh*, "after these events," denotes the conclusion of an important era. Now we usher in a new period, a new chapter in Abraham's life. The first act of the drama is finished. The second act continues from here until the *Akedah*, while the latter constitutes an act unto itself, set off with "after these events" at its beginning and conclusion—"It came to pass *ahar ha-devarim ha-eleh* that God did test Abraham" (Gen. 22:1), and "It came to pass *aharei ha-devarim ha-eleh*, that it was told Abraham, saying: Behold, Milcah, she also has borne children unto your brother Nahor" (Gen. 22:20). The fourth chapter contains the balance of Abraham's life: Sarah's death, Isaac's marriage, and then the curtain goes down on Abraham.

The curtain first went up on Abraham when God told him, "*Lekh lekha*, Go forth from your land, and from your birthplace, and from your father's house" (Gen. 12:1). Abraham went to *Eretz Yisrael* and began to climb up the ladder of success, reaching its apex with the defeat of Chedorlaomer and the biggest and strongest alliance of kings and armies. He "pursued them unto Hobah, which is on the left hand of Damascus" (Gen. 14:15), conquering the length of *Eretz Yisrael* along the way. As far as prominence, influence, and riches are concerned, kings bowed to him. "And the king of Sodom went out to meet him" (Gen. 14:17).

Interestingly, the word *berit,* "covenant," is not mentioned in the early promises pertaining to the land. "The Lord appeared unto Abram and said: Unto your seed will I give this land" (Gen. 12:7). "The Lord said to Abram after Lot left him: Lift up now your eyes and look from the place where you are northward and south . . . the entire land I will give you and to your seed forever" (Gen. 13:14–15).

Following Abraham's defeat of Chedorlaomer, the Torah begins to tell us about the second act in Abraham's life. The central motif of this act is the *berit bein ha-betarim,* the Covenant between the Parts. Only in the narrative about the *berit bein ha-betarim* does the Torah mention a covenant with Abraham stating that the land would belong to him. "In the same day the Lord made a covenant with Abram, saying, To your seed have I given this land" (Gen. 15:18). A new idea burgeons in this sentence: the covenant. A covenant means obligation, the state of being committed, the surrender of unlimited freedom. Halakhically, we call a covenant a *shtar hithayvut,* entailing the assumption of contractual duties. Of course, God is the master, whereas man is the slave, who is subordinated to the master regardless of whether a covenant is concluded. However, the covenant precipitates a state of mutuality, a commitment on the part of both master and slave. The master, as it were, also assumes duties. Any agreement presupposes surrender of freedom of action on both sides. There is a mutual promise.

The covenant ushers in a historic new experience: the faith experience, which is intrinsically a passional experience. It is a confrontation with the dreadful, the experience of the *mysterium tremendum.* "And Jacob swore by the Fear of his father Isaac" (Gen. 31:53). The covenant requires of all who join it an absolute and indomitable faith. Believing is difficult and paradoxical; the present is bleak and the future enveloped in an impenetrable mist. All hopes and expectations are in conflict with realistic, rational prognostication; they defy orderliness and the principle of causation in history.

> And he believed in the Lord; and He counted it to him for righteousness (Gen. 15:6).

> And it came to pass that, when the sun was going down, a deep sleep fell upon Abram; and lo, a dread, even a great darkness, fell upon him. And He said unto Abram, "Know of a certainty that your seed shall be a stranger in a land that is not theirs, and shall serve them; and they shall afflict them four hundred years . . ." (Gen. 15:12–13).

> And it came to pass that, when the sun went down, there was thick darkness; and behold, a smoking furnace and a flaming torch passed between these pieces (Gen. 15:17).

In the preceding quotations, we have all the elements of the historic Jewish covenantal experience. First, the toll we pay for any historical achievement in terms of blood, tears, and toil—an uncommon phenomenon in the history of other peoples; second, the feeling of dread and awe, on the one hand, and of intense hope and firm, unshakable faith with which we anticipate future events, on the other; third, the historical occurrence is a *mysterium magnum,* a great mystery, unwarranted and completely irrational if seen under the aspect of universal causation; and fourth, the awesome loneliness that the covenantal community experiences.

Do Not Fear

While Abraham experienced great material success in the first period of his life recorded in the *Humash*, the second period introduces a new motif: "And it came to pass that, when the sun was going down, a deep sleep fell upon Abram; and lo, a dread, even a great darkness, fell upon him. And He said unto Abram, 'Know of a certainty that your seed shall be a stranger in a land that is not theirs, and shall serve them; and they shall afflict them four hundred years . . .' " (Gen. 15:12–13). Abraham, you know very well that I have assigned you not just material objectives and goals. You will have to realize a great spiritual destiny. And the realization of your spiritual destiny will not be as easy as that of your material destiny. It is a long history of suffering and subjugation. Now you are a victor, but not always will your children be victors. "You shall go to your fathers in peace" (Gen. 15:15). You will not experience what I have in store for your children; you will die before that. But what the future holds for your children is not a series of successes; it is a sequence of suffering and sacrificing. God told Abraham that the spiritual destiny of the Jew would be linked up with suffering, with tragedy, and with the ability to sustain faith in the face of adversity—to expect and wait for salvation.

The introduction, *"hayah devar Hashem el Avram ba-mahazeh*, the word of the Lord came to Abram in a vision" (Gen. 15:1), is very interesting. Before that we read, *"Va-yomer Hashem*, God said to Abram, Go forth" (Gen. 12:1). Later, "The Lord appeared to Abram, *va-yomer*, and said, To your seed will I give this land" (Gen. 12:7). Here the Torah omits the term *va-yomer*, which it had used repeatedly to describe God's encounters with Abraham, and adds the word *ba-mahazeh*. *Va-yomer* means a dialogue, a conversation held face to face. God encountered Abraham and addressed Himself to him. *Devar Hashem* connotes communication from a distance; the message got to Abraham, but indirectly. God was not present. *Ba-mahazeh* means perspective, vision. *Va-yomer* is a higher medium of prophecy than *devar Hashem*. Here God was a little distant, because the message God delivered to him was one of *galut*, of exile, oppression, humiliation, and suffering. When the period of success and realization and fulfillment came to a conclusion, something happened. Before Abraham knew what God was going to tell him, he understood that the message would be different. It would be a message in which God would demand that Abraham pay the toll of the long road on which we have been traveling since his time, as we move toward the great objective which we all hope and believe will someday be attained and realized. "After these events," the period of fulfillment and realization of relative peace and success, the period of Abraham the victor, came to an end.

God says: *"Al tira Avram*, do not fear" (Gen. 15:1). Before, God spoke to him face to face; now, suddenly, it is *ba-mahazeh*, from a distance. The word reaches him from infinity, from God's transcendent abode. Abraham became apprehensive and frightened, because he recognized that the message was not one of blessing. So before delivering the message, God told him not to fear. Of course, I am not going to promise you riches and success, fulfillment and glory. But even though the message is different in nature and in substance from My previous messages, I will protect you in *galut*, in exile. *Sekharekha*, the final reward, will take hundreds and thousands of years, but the final reward is great. On that day, *ba-yom ha-hu*, everything will be fulfilled, everything will be realized.

Years later, when Jacob went down to Egypt, God appeared to him *"be-mar'ot ha-lailah"* (Gen. 46:2), not in the daytime but at night. Jacob knew this was a message of *galut*. The promissory note that Abraham had signed long before was now going to be collected, "that your seed shall be a stranger in a land that is not theirs, and shall serve them; and they shall afflict them four hundred years" (Gen. 15:13). Jacob said, *Hinneni*—I am ready for everything, even though I am very apprehensive. And right away God replied: "I am God, the God of your father" (Gen. 46:3). The message was not one of fulfillment, of success, of victory—but rather one of defeat, of a long, long sojourn in Egypt. But first of all, *al tira*, as He told Abraham, do not be afraid. Yes, it is the beginning of exile, the beginning of hundreds of years of humiliation and a wretched and defenseless existence. But through suffering and through adversity, you will become a great nation. *Sekharekha*, the final reward, is *harbeh me'od*, very great.

Count the Stars

"After these events," when God appears to Abraham in a vision, Abraham speaks of the fact that he has no offspring and "the steward of my house is my heir" (Gen. 15:3). The response is "*Vehinnei devar Hashem*" (Gen. 15:4). God interrupts him: Don't say that! If God had given an answer, the verse would have said *Va-yomer eilav*. We interrupt a person before he has a chance to finish when his question is so preposterous and unreasonable that he should not even say it. "This shall not be your heir"; the great destiny will not be handed down to Eliezer, nor will it be handed down to an Isaac trained by Eliezer. "This shall not be your heir, but he who will come forth out of your own bowels" (Gen. 15:4). He will be your own son in every sense of the word.

God took Abraham outside and told him, "Look up at the sky *u-sefor ha-kokhavim*, and try to count the stars; so shall be your seed" (Gen. 15:5). Abraham began now to calculate. I am old. Yes, God will give me a son. He will be born this year, next year, two years from now—but I will not be able to train him. It will be impossible to prepare him for the great destiny that awaits him. Abraham became a skeptic, doubting his own ability—not God's!—to prepare his son, to train and teach him. He was old and frail, physically weak, unsure of how long he was going to live.

"God brought him outside"—by his lapels, so to speak—and said, Stop brooding, Abraham! Remember the nights in

Mesopotamia when you were a boy, a young lad, how you used to watch the stars, observe them, study them, trying to find out the position of each star and each constellation, to find all the galaxies. You were so full of enthusiasm and ecstasy. You failed so many times, but you never gave up. "Look up at the sky." Remember your method of patient observation and untiring effort to discover the truth. How do you know how long you will live? Perhaps you will be as vigorous as a young man; perhaps you will be Isaac's teacher, his *rebbe,* his *melamed.* And even if you aren't able to teach Isaac, did anyone teach you? Did your father teach you? Did your mother? Did Nimrod teach you?! Still, you discovered the truth, so why should you say that no one will teach Isaac if he is born in your old age and you die? Look up, the way you were accustomed to do in your youth, and begin to count the stars. Count long and don't give up. The command is an allusion, a hint, comparing the old Abraham with the young Abraham, telling Abraham to act young.

When Abraham was a lad, when he was a shepherd and remained in the field at night, he couldn't sleep because he was restless. He could not understand the cosmos; the grandeur of the cosmic drama puzzled him. Chaldea was the land where astronomy was born. They were the first ones to describe the skies, draw maps of the heavens. Abraham counted the stars; he discovered God with the stars. When a sensitive and refined person lifts his eyes and watches the stars and the heavenly drama, he begins to think of the enormous distances and is confronted by the *ein sof*, by infinity, by endlessness itself. The sensitive soul will sense the complete worthlessness of man in comparison with infinity and will finally find God in the infinite spaces separating galaxies and stars.

God tells Abraham to count the stars. God had already used a different metaphor for the same idea, "I will make your seed as the dust of the earth: so that if a man can number, *limnot,* the dust of the earth, then shall your seed also be numbered"

(Gen. 13:16). When God spoke of the dust of the earth, He used the root *m-n-h*. When God used the stars to express to Abraham that there would be so many that it would be impossible to count them, he employed a different root, *s-f-r*. *Lispor* does not mean simply to count; it means to count and to reflect. This is the basic difference between *menoh* and *sefor*. *Limnot* means to count without an objective. *Lispor* means to count while organizing new entities, philosophizing, describing and trying to understand. *Sefor* ("count"), *saper* ("tell"), *sofer* ("scribe"), and *sefer* ("book") are all derived from one root. *Sefer Yetzirah* (1:1) points out this common derivation when it recounts that God created the world "with text (*sefer*), with number (*sefor*), and with communication (*sippur*)."

God tells Abraham not merely to count the stars, but to try to comprehend them. Can you enumerate the stars, Abraham? Can you explain the cosmic drama, the flying nebulae on the outskirts of the universe? I was with you; I stood nearby when at night in Mesopotamia you used to marvel at the mystery of the heavens. "So shall be your seed," so shall be the history of your people, of your children. Your great destiny is just as enigmatic and mysterious and incomprehensible as the great story of the heavens. Why try to rationalize it? Why complain that you are old now and unable to educate Isaac? Why question what will happen to My promises? If you had asked yourself those questions in your youth when you were counting the stars in the Mesopotamian heavens, you would never have arrived at the great conclusion, you would never have found Me, you would never have had a rendezvous with Me. "So shall be your seed"—the same principle, the same mystery, the same enigma, the same problem will be attached to your people. The story of your people is the story of the heavens; no one will ever be able to understand it. All your questions, Abraham, have this answer: "The heavens declare the glory of God, and the firmament proclaims His handiwork" (Ps. 19:2).

Actually, this chapter of Psalms has two parts, and there is no immediately apparent transition from the first part to the second. The psalm begins,

> The heavens declare the glory of God,
> and the firmament proclaims His handiwork.
> Day to day utters speech,
> and night to night expresses knowledge.
> There is no speech, nor are there words; their voice is not heard.
> Their line is gone out through all the earth,
> and their words to the end of the world.
> In them He has set a tent for the sun,
> which is like a bridegroom coming out of his chamber,
> and rejoices like a strong man to run a race.
> His going forth is from the end of the heaven,
> and His circuit to the ends of it (Ps. 19:2–7).

The first part describes the cosmos, the universe, with emphasis upon the sun. For our world, the solar system, the sun is the heroic central focus. Suddenly there is a shift:

> The Torah of the Lord is perfect, restoring the soul;
> the testimony of the Lord is sure, making wise the simple.
> The statutes of the Lord are right, rejoicing the heart;
> the commandment of the Lord is pure, enlightening the eyes.
> The fear of the Lord is clean, enduring forever;
> the judgments of the Lord are true and are righteous altogether.
> More to be desired are they than gold;
> sweeter also than honey and the honeycomb (Ps. 19:8–11).

King David is saying that God's glory manifests itself through two media. First, the medium of the cosmos. The endless energy, the dynamics of the universe, the velocity of life—that is what intrigued Abraham. Second, the medium of the Torah, the moral law, the Jewish law; it, too, tells the story of God's glory—but it is not the glory of omnipotence, not the glory of being the source of inexhaustible energy, not the glory of creation. God says to Abraham: It was the natural law that suggested My existence, My presence, to you. The regularity of phenomena, the precision that never deviates, is where you discovered Me. Now I will tell you, there is another source where I can be discovered. If you can understand it, you will be able to control the universe.

"And [Abram] believed in the Lord" (Gen. 15:6).

I Am the Lord

God now introduces Himself, so to speak, to Abraham: "I am the Lord who brought you out of Ur of the Chaldees, to give you this land to inherit it" (Gen. 15:7). Reading this, we are immediately reminded of the verse in the Ten Commandments, "I am the Lord your God, who brought you out of the land of Egypt, out of the house of slavery" (Ex. 20:2).

"Who brought you out of Ur of the Chaldees" is parallel to the phrase "who brought you out of Egypt." Interestingly, the phrase is formulated in the singular in both Exodus and Deuteronomy. This is because God makes a separate covenant with every Jew individually. Abraham was one person, so the plural form could not have been used in his case. Later, however, when six hundred thousand Jews stood at the foot of the mountain and shouted *Na'aseh ve-nishma* (Ex. 24:7), God made a covenant not with the community, not with the crowd, but with each of those Jews separately, just as He had with Abraham centuries before. The Ten Commandments are a confrontation not with six hundred thousand Jews collectively but with each one of them individually. Each of them has his own problems, each of them suffers, each is in despair. God deals with them individually. He likes the individual very much; He likes the lonely person.

The verse uses the phrase *asher hotzeitikha* and not, for example, *asher lekahtikha me-Ur Kasdim*. *Lekahtikha* means "I have taken you"; *hotzeitikha* means "I pulled you out." *Yetzi`at Mitzrayim* has a meaning that *asher lekahtikha me-eretz Mitzrayim* does not convey, and the verse itself explains it. "I am the Lord your God, who brought you out (*hotzeitikha*) of the land of Egypt, out of the house of slavery" (Ex. 20:2). I set you free, I gave you liberty. But what was the slavery in Ur of the Chaldees from which Abraham was freed? According to the Aggadah, Abraham belonged to a noble family, the aristocracy of Chaldea (*Otzar ha-Midrashim, Midrash Avraham Avinu* 3)! The answer is that any pagan, any idol-worshipper, is a slave. Even with regard to Egypt, it is not clear whether "out of the house of slavery" refers to physical bondage, to real oppression, to bricks and mortar, or to spiritual enslavement to a false way of life, to being a worshipper of idols.

The verse opens with an introduction—God's calling card, so to speak. When God addresses Himself to Abraham as the ruler of the world and creator of the universe, there is no need for Him to say who He is. He gives an order which is to be carried out. The relationship is completely objective, impersonal, and detached. But here, there is a change from the universal to the particular individual, so the first thing God does is introduce Himself. This is the beginning of the great friendship between God and Abraham. On the one hand, we are the community of the committed, and on the other hand, we are a community of equals. God befriends man, and man and God are two friends, two comrades. To be a friend, you have to introduce yourself. However, to give an order, you do not have to introduce yourself, because if you have the power to coerce someone to obey an order, you can simply force him. But God wants the Jew to feel that he is an associate, a comrade, a friend. This is the beginning of the individual relationship that will be consummated when *berit milah*, the covenant of circumcision, is given to Abraham. This was the first commandment employed by the Almighty to establish the friendship between Abraham and God.

In commenting on the Ten Commandments, Rashi (Ex. 20:2) interprets God's introduction as "I am the one who took you out of Egypt, who set you free, and who helped you become a nation; now I have come to collect. I took you out of the house of bondage not to set you free, but, on the contrary, so that you would be My servants and be committed to Me." If we apply Rashi's comment here, God is telling Abraham, "I am the creditor from whom you borrowed money in time of need. No one else trusted you; you couldn't get help from anyone. I am the only one who trusted you and had confidence in you." But the conclusion is not yet spelled out; that will come later. Why, then, did it take so long for God to reveal to Abraham how to reciprocate for the great favor and the great *hesed* God had bestowed upon him by taking him out of Ur of the Chaldees? God certainly did not wait so long after the Exodus. Only seven weeks later they reached Mount Sinai and heard God's demand for total commitment.

The answer is that in Egypt anyone could recognize God's grace. They were taken out of physical bondage, were set free after having been slaves for hundreds of years. Having felt the oppressor's whip on their backs, having seen their children drowned in the Nile, they understood very well what freedom means in comparison to slavery. There was no need for meditation to understand what God had done for them. But Abraham was not in a "house of slavery" in any physical sense. On the contrary, he was taken out of a rich, aristocratic home, in an ancestral land to which he was bound by hundreds of threads. God suddenly told him to become a wanderer, an immigrant, a stranger, a vagabond, a nomad—worse off than he had been before. Therefore, God could not immediately demand reciprocity. Abraham had to understand what God wanted him to become, what idol worship was, and what his new life meant. There was a need for thoughts to ripen and for understanding to become clear. This process of education helped Abraham comprehend in retrospect what God had done for him, how he had been spiritually a slave with no inner freedom. When God knew that Abraham finally understood, He introduced Himself as the one who had taken him out of Ur of the Chaldees.

There is another interpretation of the introductory phrase in the Decalogue. Rashi asks: Why do we say: "I am the Lord your God, who brought you out of the land of Egypt" (Ex. 20:2)? He explains: God revealed Himself to them at the Red Sea as a strong young warrior, and at Sinai He revealed Himself as a merciful old man. Although the media of revelation differ, and sometimes you see Me in the form of a warrior, and other times in the form of a mature, experienced teacher, do not say that there are two gods. It is the same God who appeared to you at the Red Sea as a young warrior and here at Sinai as a mature teacher.

God sometimes acts like a strong young warrior and sometimes like a merciful old man. The same is also true with regard to Abraham. Abraham's career was one of fulfillment. He came as a stranger, a wanderer, an alien—and he became rich and wealthy, gained influence, and occupied a prominent place in society. The Hittites said to him: "You are a mighty prince among us" (Gen. 23:6). God was now about to announce to Abraham not only fulfillment but also something else. Abraham felt that the land would not be so easily given to him, that there would be a long road to travel before he possessed *Eretz Yisrael*. "And he said, Lord God, how shall I know that I shall inherit it?" (Gen. 15:8). When God informed him that he would have progeny, "he believed in the Lord" (Gen. 15:6) and did not ask anything; but when told that the land would be his, he asked for a sign. As a matter of fact, we know it was four hundred years in Egypt before the daybreak of fulfillment, a long night of slavery and oppression, a night of *galut Mitzrayim*.

Indeed, no one's life is a long, unbroken series of fulfillments. There are certain times when our lives make sense to us, and we feel nostalgic whenever we reminisce about them. But other times in our lives make no sense at all. All we can do is bend our heads to accept God's wisdom. There is no other way. This is also true of Jewish history. Some periods of our history make sense. We see fulfillment, we can trace the footsteps of God, we can feel His presence. However, some periods are bleak and frightening, such as the years between 1939 and 1945, that terrible period unique in Jewish history, a time of total *hester panim*, a total "hiding of the face."

Now Abraham's period of fulfillment is coming to an end and a new period begins to dawn. "And lo, a dread, even a great darkness, fell upon him. And He said unto Abram, Know of a certainty that your seed shall be a stranger in a land that is not theirs" (Gen. 15:12–13). Abraham does not understand. If God is kind and is with me, he asks, why do I have to go through *galut Mitzrayim* in order to get to *Eretz Yisrael*? Couldn't the land of Canaan be given us right away; is the winding road really necessary?

God says: On the one hand, I am the God of mercy and kindness. I helped you; you prospered and lived in abundance, and in a few days you defeated all your enemies. But now begins the period of waiting and expectation, of faith and prayer. You won't be able to defeat your enemies; the enemies will defeat you. But don't think that you have actually lost Me; I will be with you nonetheless. I am the same God.

Here is a historical contradiction, the transition from fulfillment to a destiny of waiting, from prominence and freedom and power to slavery and oppression. These fluctuations in Jewish history cannot be understood, but no Jew has ever despaired. God is there when man is triumphant, when man lives in luxury, when man is free—and He is the same God when man is suffering, when he lives in poverty, when he is in need.

Abraham understood right away, and he said, "*Ba-mah eida,* how will I know?" (Gen. 15:8). *Ba-mah eida* is not a request for a sign or miracle to prove the veracity of God's statement. Abraham understood that God is the same even if his descendants' destiny was changing, even though their fate was being transformed from one of prominence to slavery. He asked: Whereby will I know that the time is right for me to take *Eretz Yisrael*? What do You expect me to give you for that?

God responded, "Bring me three heifers and three female goats, and three rams and a turtledove, and a young pigeon. And he took to Him all these, and He divided them in the middle" (Gen. 15:9-10). It was God who divided them. He explained to Abraham: There will come a time when the Jewish people will be divided, torn apart by suffering, by oppression, by humiliation. The birds of prey will swoop down. They will think that because the nation has been torn apart and divided, it is dead and cannot be resurrected. "Your seed shall be a stranger in a land that is not theirs, and shall serve them; and they shall afflict them four hundred years . . . But in the fourth generation they shall come here again" (Gen. 15:13, 16). Abraham took three heifers, three goats, and three rams—the three generations that would die in Egypt in abject poverty, slavery, and oppression, that would not live to see the day of redemption. "But in the fourth generation they shall come here again" (Gen. 15:16). Three generations will die, their hopes will not be fulfilled, their faith will not be vindicated. Only the fourth generation will see the Messiah, the redeemer Moses.

This is basically the Jewish approach to evil. We have never answered the question of why evil exists. There is no answer. Every philosopher who has tried to write a theodicy has failed, including Maimonides in his *Guide of the Perplexed*. But the Jew always asks: How am I supposed to act in the face of evil, when confronted by evil?

Willy-nilly, whether or not we ask the question, there is no way to get away from the confrontation with evil. There is no way to protect oneself from this encounter. We confronted evil in its ugliest form during the Hitler era. I have met many Holocaust survivors. Some lost everything—their faith in God, their faith in themselves, their sense of dignity. For some, suffering was a crucible in which they attained great heights, and for some, suffering was degrading and spiritually annihilating. Many could no longer believe "I am the Lord who brought you out of Ur of the Chaldees," and if you lose God in times of trouble, even in times of individual trouble, you lose yourself as well. That is why God told Abraham, I want you to remember during the long night of dread, during the long night of human wretchedness and failure, that "I am the Lord who brought you out of Ur of the Chaldees." There were better times before, and finally the day will arrive when better times return.

Conquest and Inheritance

God promises to give the land to Abraham *lerishtah* (Gen. 15:7), and Abraham asks how shall I know *ki irashennah* (Gen. 15:8). *Lerishtah* is usually translated as "to inherit," but Abraham did not inherit the land. Terah, his father, never owned the land. Abraham was the first beneficiary of the grant.

In truth, *lerishtah* has a double connotation: inherit and conquer. "Behold, the Lord your God has set the land before you; *aleh resh*" (Deut. 1:21). *Resh* does not mean "inherit"; it means "take it" or "conquer it."

What is new in this message to Abraham, when God promises the land *lerishtah*? After all, the message that the land would belong to him had been delivered to Abraham when he had arrived from Haran and from Egypt: "To your seed *etten*, I shall give this land" (Gen. 12:7); "All the land that you see, to you *ettenenah*, I shall give it, and to your seed" (Gen. 13:15). *Ettenenah* means "I give a grant, a *mattanah*." Abraham apparently imagined that the land would be passed to him on a silver platter. The seven nations that inhabited the land would all come to him and say, "You are a prince of God in our midst" (Gen. 23:6), take the land.

Suddenly, Abraham got a different message, one that changed the whole panorama. Things began to look gloomy and dark. *Lerishtah*, you will have to do the conquering; it will not be offered to you. I will not break *tiv'o shel olam*, the natural causal nexus. I will not make people surrender the land to you voluntarily, because this has never happened and will never happen. You will have to struggle for it. The thirty-one kings did not surrender land to Joshua. He was engaged in a bitter seven-year fight. The State of Israel has been fighting longer.

It is not only the land that we must conquer. There is something else, something just as important as the land and perhaps even more significant. It was given to us as a gift but we have to struggle for it, quest for it, fight for it, and conquer it. I am referring, of course, to the Torah. The Torah was given to us, but that does not mean that knowledge of the Torah was bestowed upon every one of us as a gift. *Pirkei Avot* (6:6) enumerates forty-eight prerequisites for becoming erudite and knowledgeable, the most important of which is *yegi'ah*, hard work and diligence to the point that one becomes fatigued. Creative Torah scholarship requires complete dedication, unconditional commitment, full absorption, making Torah one's sole interest. If the Torah is just one interest among many, then even if you are very intelligent or have some knowledge about certain aspects, you cannot be a great scholar. The Torah must be shifted from the periphery to the center. This is true of every branch of scholarship. You cannot be a great mathematician unless you live, eat, and sleep mathematics; all the more so regarding Torah. The Torah and the land were given us *lerishtah*. The only difference is that in order to conquer the land, we have to fight others; in order to conquer the Torah, we have to fight ourselves—our laziness, our tardiness, our inclination to procrastinate. We have to fight for self-discipline of thought and habit. God gives man an opportunity—but only an opportunity. Man must exploit the opportunity and develop his own skills and his own talents.

Returning to our passage, it is also possible to interpret *ler-ishtah* in the sense of inheritance. There is a fundamental difference between something acquired by gift or purchase and something acquired by inheritance. Aside from the halakhic distinction, there is also a psychological distinction between the two, between what the Torah calls *sedeh miknah* and *sedeh ahuzzah* (Lev. 27:16, 22). A *sedeh miknah* is a field that was acquired by gift or purchase. A *sedeh ahuzzah* is a field or an estate inherited from one's father, and by that father from his father, and so on, going back to the partition of the land. A *sedeh miknah* that was sold need not be redeemed. But a man who sells a *sedeh ahuzzah* must redeem it if he is in a position to do so. If not, his next of kin or relatives should help redeem it. "If your brother should be impoverished and sell from his *ahuzzah*, the next of kin should come and redeem what his brother sold" (Lev. 25:25). Psychologically, it is not easy to part with a *sedeh ahuzzah* because it was inherited and can be traced back through many generations to the partition of the land.

Naboth the Jezreelite had a vineyard next to the palace. When Ahab asked him to sell this plot in exchange for land of higher quality, because he wanted to plant a vegetable garden, Naboth refused, protesting that he did not wish to "give the inheritance, *nahalah*, of my fathers to you" (I Kings 21:3). One must not sell something that was dear to one's father and forefathers. (*Ahuzzah*, *morashah*, and *nahalah* are synonyms.) Biblical man could not part easily with the *nahalah*, with the homestead. (Interestingly, we read, "Pardon our iniquity and our sin, and take us for Your inheritance, *u-nehaltanu*" [Ex. 34:9]. Take us into Your possession, the way a person takes a *nahalah* into his possession. This means that God can never separate Himself from us. No inducement could persuade Naboth to give up his *nahalah,* and that is what we ask from God with respect to ourselves.)

Abraham asks, *"Ba-mah eida,* by what shall I know that I shall inherit it?" (Gen. 15:8). *"Eida"* here means much more than "know." We read, "And God heard their groaning, and God remembered His covenant with Abraham, Isaac, and Jacob, *va-yeda Elokim*" (Ex. 2:24–25). *Va-yeda Elokim* means that He experienced their travail, their pain, their suffering, their humiliation. It is complete sympathy, compassion and involvement. Similarly, "*Ki yadati* their sorrows" (Ex. 3:7) means "I felt their pain." "Adam *yada* Eve his wife" (Gen. 4:1) means that he loved her and they were intimate. Abraham's question means, How will I love the land so much? How do you expect me to establish an eternal bond between myself and the land, such that it will become a homestead passed on for all generations? After all, God had told him to leave his native land, to leave his ancestral home, to abandon his family. So apparently the bond between a person and the land of his ancestors is not sacred. Now God suddenly tells him that he is to remember the promised land and pass it on to his children; this will be his testament, his will, and nothing in the world can sever the bond. It is sacred; no human hand can touch it, he will fight for it now and over thousands of years. How, asks Abraham, do you expect me and my descendants to cling to the land, incapable of severing the bonds?

God's answer is to take a heifer, a goat, a ram, a pigeon, and a turtledove. A heifer is a young cow, the goat and the ram both belong to the category of sheep, and the pigeon and turtledove to the category of birds. These are the three classes the Torah has designated as those from which one can bring a *korban*, so the selection covers *in toto* the area of sacrifices. Abraham's deep commitment to the land will be based on sacrifice. You do not appreciate something if you do not have to fight for it, if you do not suffer and sacrifice in order to get it. God rewards us in accordance with our efforts (*Avot* 5:26). The most distinctive feature of the Jewish people is its readiness to sacrifice. The whole history of the Jewish people is made up of sacrifice and martyrdom. I am speaking not only about the martyrdoms in the time of the Crusades or Chmielnicki, when Jews chose to incur death rather than accept Christianity or desert God. It is more than that; it is the everyday sacrifice of the Jew in so many ways! We have no concept now of what Jews went through in order to maintain their identity and survive spiritually. But we won the battle because we knew the secret of sacrificial action.

God tells Abraham, *Yado'a teda*, You will be intensely dedicated to the land, *ki*, because "your seed shall be a stranger in a land that is not theirs," because you will not get the land immediately and will have to wait a long time for it. They will be slaves and ill-treated for four hundred years. Throughout the dark night of *galut*, you will have only one dream, one vision, one aspiration, one hope: to get back to *Eretz Yisrael*! "Next year in Jerusalem!" And after you return to *Eretz Yisrael*, I assure you that you will be deeply in love with the land. It will be an eternal love, not just a passing affair.

That is exactly what we emphasize in the Passover Haggadah:

> Originally our fathers were idolaters; but now the Omnipresent has brought us close to His service, as it states: "And Joshua said to all the nation: Thus says God, the Lord of Israel, Your fathers always lived across the river—Terah, the father of Abraham and Nahor, and they served other gods. And I took your father Abraham from beyond the river, and I led him throughout the entire land of Canaan. I increased his seed and gave him Isaac. I gave Jacob and Esau to Isaac, and I gave Mount Se'ir to Esau to inherit, and Jacob and his sons descended to Egypt" (Joshua 24:2–4).

Eretz Yisrael was not given immediately to Jacob the way Mount Se'ir was turned over to Esau. The Torah tells us how Esau moved from Canaan to Mount Se'ir the way one moves from one apartment to another. "And Esau took his wives, and his sons, and his daughters, and all the persons of his house, and his cattle, and all his beasts, and all his substance, which he had acquired in the land of Canaan; and went into another country away from his brother Jacob" (Gen. 36:6). But in order for Jacob and his children to get the land of Israel, they first had to go down to Egypt.

God or Abraham took the animals "and divided them in the midst and laid each half against the others, but the birds he divided not" (Gen. 15:10). The bird is a symbol of having the ability to rise from the ground into endless space, soaring high. The Jewish spirit has never been defeated. Many times, we were actually cut to pieces, but even then the Jewish spirit soared. One generation will die in exile, a second generation, a third generation, "but the birds he divided not."

"And the bird of prey came down upon the carcasses" (Gen. 15:11). It was not one bird of prey that swooped down upon us. There were many, and there are still birds of prey that swoop down on us. "And Abraham chased them away." It is not only the concrete Abraham who lived thousands of years ago who did so. It is also Abraham the symbol, Abraham the revolutionary. It is the Abraham who could wait and patiently expect a son at the age of a hundred. Here he received a prophecy, a tragic revelation, a message of suffering, of martyrdom and frustration, and of endless waiting, four hundred years for redemption from slavery and oppression. But, on the other hand, the *berit bein ha-betarim* conveys a message not so much of redemption as of spiritual survival, of being able to wait endlessly until the final day arrives. "And He said unto Abram, Know of a certainty that your seed shall be a stranger in a land that is not theirs, and shall serve them; and they shall afflict them four hundred years, and also that nation, whom they shall serve, will I judge; and afterwards shall they come out *bi-rekhush gadol*, with great substance" (Gen. 15:13–14).

Rekhush gadol does not mean a few silver cups borrowed from the Egyptians. It was not gold, not silver, not cloth, but a spiritual treasure: the experience of suffering: both suffering, on the one hand, and resistance, tenacity, and heroic strength on the other. This is symbolized by having the three animals cut up in the center—this is complete enslavement, oppression, martyrdom—and still have the birds soaring high.

"And it came to pass that, when the sun was going down, a deep sleep fell upon Abram; and lo, a dread, even a great darkness, fell upon him" (Gen. 15:12). This is the experience of *galut.* Abraham experienced the dread of the *galut,* but he did not personally experience the consolation of the enemy's final defeat and our emergence as victors. This is our destiny, which has repeated itself many times. It is still valid; it is still a part of our contemporary reality.

At the *berit bein ha-betarim,* the covenant was limited to our historical experience. It was concluded between the Almighty and Abraham as the representative and father of a community, a people that makes history. When the precept of circumcision was later revealed to Abraham, the covenant was extended to the individual. His own way of life was transformed into a unique covenantal mode of existence.

> The Lord appeared to Abram, and said to him, I am the Almighty God; walk before Me, and be perfect. And I will make My covenant between Me and you (Gen. 17:1–2).

> As for Me, behold, My covenant is with you, and you shall be a father of many nations. Neither shall your name any more be called Abram, but your name shall be Abraham; for a father of many nations have I made you (Gen. 17:4–5).

> And I will establish My covenant between Me and you and your seed after you in their generations to be a God to you, and to your seed after you. And I will give to you,

and to your seed after you, the land where you are a stranger, all the land of Canaan, for an everlasting possession; and I will be their God (Gen. 17:7–8).

This is My covenant, which you shall keep. Every male child among you shall be circumcised (Gen. 17:10).

With circumcision, another mission was assigned to Abraham: the formation and education of a covenantal community, a community that would be close to God and would follow a new way of life, an enigmatic *modus existentiae*, a special relationship to God. Abraham was burdened with a double mission: to civilize and teach the universal community, and at the same time to create a new community by teaching one boy, Isaac.

❧ The Visit

The Lord Appeared to Him

*P*arashat Lekh Lekha speaks about promise, but the road leading from promise to fulfillment is a tortuous one. In *Parashat Va-yera,* we confront the beginning of the fulfillment of Abraham's destiny, at least insofar as the birth of Isaac is concerned. "The Lord appeared to him, *va-yera eilav Hashem,* in the groves of Mamre, as he sat at the entrance of his tent in the heat of the day" (Gen. 18:1).

What first attracts our attention to this verse are the parallel verses of God's appearing to Abraham: "The Lord appeared to Abram, and said, *va-yomer*" (Gen. 12:7). After Abraham won the battle with the kings, "The word of God came to him in a vision *lemor,* saying" (Gen. 15:1). Again there was a message, God told him something. And then, "When Abram was ninety nine years old, the Lord appeared, *va-yera,* to Abram, and He said to him, *va-yomer eilav*" (Gen. 17:1). He appeared to him, He revealed Himself and told him something, commanded him or promised him or enlightened him—a message was delivered. But here there is no *va-yomer.* What was the purpose of the revelation, what objective was God seeking; what did He tell him? There was no message. Moreover, none of the preceding verses describing God's appearances to Abraham use the pronoun *eilav*. Abraham is always referred to by name. But here we have "*Va-yera eilav Hashem*, the Lord appeared to him." The pronoun *eilav* refers back to Abraham, who is mentioned in the preceding chapter. But why does the verse relate this revelation to the story recorded in the last chapter and not start *de novo,* from scratch?

Rashi says: "*Va-yera eilav,* He appeared to him in order to visit the sick." God paid Abraham a sick call because he was in pain after his circumcision. Rabbi Hama ben Hanina said that it was the third day following the circumcision, when one suffers severe pain, and the Almighty appeared to ask about his state of health (*Bava Metzi'a* 86b). Abraham was in need, and God came to visit him. There is no *va-yomer*, no message, no command, no law, no promise. God simply came to see him. If two individuals are close friends, sharing a sense of intimacy and companionship, then one of them need not have a message to deliver in order to walk into the other's home. That is where Martin Buber made his biggest mistake. Conversation or dialogue is not the highest form of friendship. Once a conversation comes to an end, there is nothing else to do but leave the house. But the highest form of friendship does not require words. I do not have to tell my friend why I came to see him. I just come, because I like to be present in his home. This usually happens between husband and wife, between brother and sister or parent and child. Except in our halakhic studies, my father talked very little to me; he never confided in me. But he wanted me to be around, because he liked me. There was no need for words, for an exchange of remarks. Why does a mother like to have her baby sleep in her room, or in a room next to her? It is not simply because of the safety of the baby. The mere feeling that the baby is nearby gives her satisfaction.

Before this visit, the relationship between God and Abraham was a formal one; it did not involve friendship. There was a contractual relationship between employer and employee, between master and servant. Every *va-yera* was accompanied by a *va-yomer*. But after Abraham was circumcised and the covenant established, there was a new intimacy, a new kind of friendship—one that did not have to be expressed in words, that did not need speech or a message. Familiarity has changed into friendship, where the *va-yomer* is completely superfluous. The purpose of visiting is not to tell him anything, but just to see him, to listen to his voice. God came because Abraham was ill, but even if Abraham had been well, God would have been there.

Now we understand why *eilav* is used. As long as the relationship is a formal one, it is guided by the rules of courtesy. Formality requires mentioning the name. But when we visit a friend, there is no need for the name. Furthermore, in the Bible, the verb and the subject are usually not separated. If *va-yera* is the verb and God is the subject, the verse should have read *va-yera Hashem eilav*, not *va-yera eilav Hashem*. By reversing the subject and the object, the Torah means to emphasize that Abraham was very close to God, that God longed to see him. He felt lonely without Abraham, so to speak. He wanted to see him, just as a mother wants to see her baby, or a father his child. There is no need for *va-yomer*; God simply wanted to be near Abraham. That is why Isaiah (41:8) calls him *Avraham ohavi,* "My beloved." Up to this point we have been reading the story of *Avraham avdi,* Abraham the servant of God. From *Parashat Va-yera* on is a new story; a new tale is introduced, the story of Abraham the friend of God.

Let us compare God's revelation to Abraham in the *berit bein ha-betarim* with this visit. We read in *Lekh Lekha,* "And it came to pass that, when the sun was going down, a deep sleep fell upon Abram; and lo, a dread, even a great darkness, fell upon him. And He said unto Abram, Know of a certainty that your seed shall be a stranger in a land that is not theirs" (Gen. 15:12–13). When God reveals Himself to Abraham here, the story is told in three words: "*Va-yera eilav Hashem.*" The elements of fear and fright, the overpowering sleep, the loss of faculties in the earlier encounter with the Almighty are not mentioned.

Apparently there are two kinds of revelation, and the contrast between them is huge. The experience of revelation as described in *Lekh Lekha* is accompanied by fright and horror. Man is completely awed and feels crushed by the impact of his confrontation with the Almighty. Confused and frightened, he finds himself standing on the brink of infinity, which is about to rob him of his existential autonomy and dignity. The encounter with God means the end of man, for he cannot stand up in the presence of God without losing his own identity. When finitude is added to infinity, the result is infinity. If man stands too close to God, man disappears.

That man is frightened by the presence of God is well known to us from the Bible. For instance, David says: "Where shall I go from Your spirit, or where shall I flee from Your presence?" (Ps. 139:7). This is the *pahad* or *yir'at Elokim* that man feels in the presence of God. Consider an ignorant person—one who knows that he is ignorant—meeting with the greatest of scholars. He has a feeling of humility and worthlessness that will ultimately be translated into an experience of fright or even non-existence. Man loses his human dignity when he comes close to the Master of the Universe because he compares his existence with the eternal, infinite existence of the Almighty, and this leads to fear of God. This is exactly what transpired at the *berit bein ha-betarim*. Abraham completely lost his self-worth and dignity when he was overpowered by the presence of God.

The revelation described in *Va-yera* is more of a redemptive experience, cathartic and joyous. Man is no longer frightened by the appearance of the Almighty; on the contrary, it gives him a sense of unshakable security and confidence. "The Lord is my shepherd, I shall not want; in lush meadows He lays me down" (Ps. 23:1–2). When I am close to God, I feel safe. I know that He will take care of all my needs. I feel His hand on my neck, just as the sheep feels the hand of the shepherd; I lack nothing.

"Surely goodness and mercy shall follow me all the days of my life" (Ps. 23:6). When God accompanies me, I do not have to be afraid of anything. When God appears to man and receives him like an old friend, man is elated, invigorated, and happy. He feels secure and safe.

The two attributes we ascribe to God, *ha-gadol ve-ha-nora*, represent these two experiences. *Ha-nora* means that He is inaccessible, that it is hard to draw near to Him. However, when the revelation of the *Shekhinah* is the experience of God's love, then it is *ha-gadol*—God takes in the whole world. *Ha-gadol* means *hesed*, complete *bittahon*, confidence and faith in the Almighty. As a matter of fact, Rosh Ha-Shanah and Yom Kippur represent different God experiences. Rosh Ha-Shanah evokes the painful, numinous experience—"You are holy and Your name is *nora*." It is a day of *din*, judgment, when we experience God as the King. Yom Kippur, however, is a day of *rahamim*, mercy, when we experience God as a loving father: "Fortunate are you, O Israel! Before whom are you purified? Who purifies you? Before your Father in Heaven" (Mishnah *Yoma* 8:9). The two experiences together represent the total religious experience. Abraham first experienced revelation in numinous God in terms of fright and awe. The second revelation was experienced in terms of love and *hesed*—as cathartic and redemptive.

What happened that changed the experience of *ha-nora* to that of *ha-gadol*? The change was due to the introduction of a new idea into the relationship between God and man. I refer to *milah*, which entails the idea of *berit*, of covenant. When God informed Abraham about the Egyptian servitude, Abraham was just a human being—a great human being, but not a party to a covenant. He met God the way any other human being would have, with feelings of awe and fear. Here, however, God visits Abraham after he has joined the covenantal community and submitted himself to circumcision, which is the sign and symbol of the covenant. If a Jew is uncircumcised, not only has he not fulfilled the mitzvah of circumcision and thus is subject to *hiyyuv karet*, excision—but he also lacks something of *kedushat Yisrael*, the sanctity of Israel. He is a Jew, but not a *ben berit*, not a member of the covenant. (These two dimensions of *milah* are reflected in the two blessings that we pronounce upon it: one on the mitzvah of *milah* per se, and one on entering into Abraham's covenant.) A Jew has sanctity as a descendant of the founders of the covenantal society; this is the *kedushat avotekha*. But he needs *berit milah* for *kedushat atzmekha*, which can be formulated as acceptance of the covenantal obligations that Abraham took upon himself. It is a commitment to a community consisting of God and man. We are committed to God, and He demands compliance from us. Within the covenantal community, God addresses Himself to man in a natural way; He engages man in a dialogue. Indeed, within the covenantal community man and God are friends. This is why Nahmanides (Gen. 48:15) interprets Jacob's phrase "the God who has been *ro'eh oti* all my life" not as "the God who has been my shepherd," as most commentators explain, but rather as "the God who has been my *re'ah*, my friend."

The experience of intimacy with God was made possible by the creation of the covenantal community. Hasidism accepts the idea that God's transcendence, His remoteness from the world, is due to the first sin, *het ha-kadmon*. When God created the world, He wanted *ikkar Shekhinah be-tahtonim* (Gen. Rabbah 19:7), that He would reside within the universe, among people, and be intimate with them. But the sin interfered with God's inscrutable will and made Him leave this world. "And they heard the voice of the Lord God walking" (Gen. 3:8) means that He was departing from the garden, from this world. Adam and Eve heard the footsteps of the Holy One walking out of the universe. God broke the intimate relationship that was supposed to be realized by Adam. The purpose of the covenant concluded with Abraham was to restore the intimacy that God wanted to prevail between Him and man. At Sinai, the covenant embraced not only one individual but the whole community. The ideal is to extend the covenant even further, to the rest of the world.

If I may introduce a personal note, many times I feel very close to God. I feel His hand on my shoulder. This happens not only during *tefillah*, prayer, but during *talmud Torah*, when I am studying. I may study at night alone in the room, delving into a passage in Tosafot that on its face makes no sense. When I restore the coherence of the Tosafot and succeed in conceptualizing the text, I feel happy not only because this is creative work, but because I feel the presence of *Ha-Kadosh Barukh Hu* over my shoulder, looking into the book, at the text. I then feel that all my prayers will be implemented if I *daven* properly. Our experience of the Holy One should be intimate, as if I can touch Him and feel Him looking at me. Thus God came to Abraham *lish'ol bi-shlomo*, to inquire after his health, to show friendship and involvement.

Rashi (Gen. 18:1) cites a strange midrash here: " 'In the groves of Mamre'—since Mamre had advised Abraham concerning circumcision, God revealed Himself to Abraham in his estate" (Gen. Rabbah 42:8). Abraham, the devoted servant of God, did not need Mamre's advice; I understand it to mean rather that Mamre encouraged him. The reason he needed encouragement is to be found in a midrash concerning God's command to Abraham to circumcise himself: "Abraham said, Before I was circumcised, people would come and attach themselves to me; now that I will be circumcised, will You tell me that they will still come and attach themselves to me? The Holy One answered, ['I am *E-l Sha-ddai*':] It is sufficient (*dai*) that I am your God; it is sufficient that I am your patron" (Gen. Rabbah 46:3).

Milah is the symbol of the patriarchic covenant, the *berit avot*. While the Sinaitic covenant has 613 *mitzvot*, which entail a unique way of life, the patriarchic covenant has just one—but it is one that sets the Jew apart. The patriarchic covenant means simply that the Jewish people has a unique and singular historical destiny. Abraham feared that when he would circumcise himself, people would boycott him; they would avoid him because he is different and unique. God answered: You are right, Abraham; your loneliness will be intensified, but you will have Me as your friend and protector. Apparently, Mamre was an exception to this. He encouraged Abraham, telling him: Whether you will be circumcised or not, you will not lose my friendship.

Abraham "sat at the entrance of his tent" (Gen. 18:1). It is not necessary to renounce the world in order to be close to God. A person can be within the world, be a part of the world, be engaged in human affairs, sitting in front of his tent, not somewhere in a retreat, in isolation, in a cave, in a cell, locked up and isolated after long days of prayer and devotion. Abraham was busy with the daily chores, his everyday affairs. But if you attend to your everyday affairs in a manner satisfactory to God, you have an encounter with the Holy One, blessed be He.

"Ve-hu yoshev, he sat at the entrance of his tent," the verse says. Yoshev is in the present tense, but the vav is missing, allowing the word to be read as yashav, in the past tense. Rashi quotes here a strange midrash: "Abraham was seated and wanted to get up, but God told him, Remain seated and I shall stand. And the fact that you remain seated symbolizes something that will happen in the future" (Gen. Rabbah 48:7). Noting that judges must sit when they accept testimony and when they render the decision, Rashi then continues, "Says God, I shall stand, and the judges will be sitting, as the verse says, 'God stands in the congregation of God, [in the midst of judges He judges]' (Ps. 82:1)." What does Rashi want to convey?

When an important, dignified person comes to us, we rise and receive him standing. The host stands at the door, receiving his guests. The Holy One came to visit Abraham, so Abraham jumped up from his seat. He was in pain and had just had major surgery, but he jumped up right away. God said, You are making a mistake, Abraham. You consider yourself the host and Me the guest. The opposite is true; I am the host and you are the guest. I am receiving you, not in your tent, but in My tent. It is My tent; nothing is yours, so remain seated. And the same is true in every court. Judaism has never accepted the concept of judging people. How can a human being who is a sinner, who is just as imperfect as the accused person in the dock—what right does he have to render judgment? "Judgment belongs to God" (Deut. 1:17). But the Torah allows judgment, because if human beings were not permitted to judge their fellow men, anarchy would prevail. Nonetheless, the judge, whoever he may be, must always remember that he is just a plenipotentiary, an agent or a messenger from the Almighty, who is the real judge. "God stands in the congregation of God, in the midst of judges He judges" (Ps. 82:1). He is the owner. He is the master. We are just guests and tenants who will be invited to take a seat while God the host remains standing.

Hospitality

There are two ways of understanding the verse, "The Lord appeared to him in the groves of Mamre, as he sat in the entrance of his tent in the heat of the day" (Gen. 18:1). Some, like Rashbam, see this verse as a general statement that is elaborated upon and explained in the verse that follows: "And he raised his eyes and looked, and lo, three men stood by him; and when he saw them, he ran to meet them from the tent door, and bowed himself to the ground" (Gen. 18:2). The divine revelation ("The Lord appeared to him") took place in the form of three angels coming to visit Abraham.

The other view, which is the position of *Hazal*, is that God came as a friend without delivering a message. In verse 1, God appeared to Abraham, who had an encounter with the Almighty. In verse 2, something else happened: Abraham saw three men standing nearby, ran to meet them, and bowed to the ground. *Hazal* emphasized this, because a great moral is implied. Abraham felt the Divine Presence and suddenly noticed three travelers whom he did not know; they were not acquaintances or friends. What was Abraham supposed to do?

As *Hazal* describe it, this was one of the tests Abraham had to pass to show that he was worthy of becoming the father of the nation. Should he tell the Holy One to wait or, on the contrary, not pay attention to the three travelers and attend to his God? How would we act? Here is an encounter with God—the highest experience of which a human being can ever dream, the highest form of bliss. What more could a human being ask for, if not to be close to the Eternal? But when Abraham saw the travelers, he ran to meet them, prostrated himself, and said, "*Adonai*, if now I have found favor in Your eyes, do not pass by your servant" (Gen. 18:3). One opinion in *Hazal* interprets *adonai* as "my masters," referring to the travelers, and another opinion reads it as a holy name addressed to God (*Shevu'ot* 35b). According to the latter reading, Abraham ran to meet the travelers, but before he left he turned to God and said, "My Lord, please wait for me. You came to visit me. I enjoy Your visit. I am very satisfied. You are very welcome here. But now I am busy, I have no time. I have to attend to the travelers." Then he turned around and addressed the travelers, "Let a little water, I pray you, be fetched, and wash your feet" (Gen. 18:4).

Thus *Hazal* said that to receive lonely travelers on a hot day and give them water to drink, tell them to wash up and serve them food, is greater than being in the company and presence of the Almighty (*Shabbat* 127a). When the travelers bade Abraham farewell "and went toward Sodom"—this was after several hours, who knows how long?—"Abraham stood yet before the Lord" (Gen. 18:22). God waited for him, and Abraham was still in His presence.

Why is *hakhnasat orehim* so emphasized here? There are many ways to practice kindness. The cruelty of Sodom is portrayed in terms of cruelty to guests and strangers; in contrast, Abraham's kindness expressed itself particularly in *hakhnasat orehim*. Bear in mind that *hakhnasat orehim* is often for the poor. A rich man is in no need of hospitality; he can find an inn or a place to stay. Yet *hakhnasat orehim* differs from *tzedakah,* or material help to others, in a crucial way. When one gives *tzedakah*, it demonstrates sympathy, but not a philosophy of human equality holding that all Jews are *benei melakhim*, princes, regardless of differences in wealth or knowledge. *Hakhnasat orehim*, however, demonstrates full human equality, the fact that every being has his own dignity and is just as important as any other. It is much easier to give someone money and send him away than to invite him under your own roof. If I invite him in, that means that no matter what his station in life, I am treating him with respect, as an equal. *Hakhnasat orehim* is symbolic of our personal relationships, and that is why the Torah gave us this picture of Abraham.

Praying for Sodom

Three travelers came: one to announce the birth of Isaac, one to destroy Sodom, and the third to heal Abraham (*Bava Metzi'a* 86b). Rashi (18:2), quoting the Midrash, explains that each angel is given only one assignment (Gen. Rabbah 50:2). (This is also true of human beings; we are each given but one assignment.) Let us understand the connection between the three angels.

> God said, Will I hide from Abraham what I am going to do, seeing that Abraham shall surely become a great and mighty nation, and all the nations of the earth shall be blessed in him? For I know him, that he will command his children, and his household after him, and they shall keep the way of the Lord, to do righteousness and judgment; that the Lord may bring upon Abraham that which He has spoken of him. And the Lord said, Because the cry of Sodom and Gomorrah is great, and because their sin is very grievous . . . (Gen. 18:17–20).

Sodom was prosperous and had "dust of gold" (Job 28:6). As long as Sodom prospered, Abraham's doctrines, sermonizing, and preaching meant nothing. One cannot preach goodness and kindness if *malkhut ha-rish 'ah*, the kingdom of evil, is rich and powerful. One cannot gain converts for an idea if its opponents, no matter how bad they are, prosper—are strong, respected, feared. An angel came to announce the birth of Isaac—in other words, the continuation of Abraham's heritage. But Sodom's existence contradicts everything Abraham has said. Abraham preaches equality, kindness, charity, and hospitality; Sodom laughs and scoffs at these ideas. Sodom is prosperous and mighty; Abraham is just one person. So when the angel came to tell Abraham that Isaac will be born and that his hopes will be fulfilled, another angel accompanied him to say that not only will Isaac be his successor, but his powerful opponent will be destroyed. This will strengthen his position, and people will begin to realize that evil does not pay. That is why the two angels came together.

And here the Torah tells us something important about Abraham. If we had been in his place, we would simply have prostrated ourselves and thanked God for destroying the kingdom of evil so that our task would be simplified. But Abraham pleaded for Sodom, knowing that its survival meant his own defeat. He was ready to accept defeat in order to give Sodom an opportunity to reform and restore itself. Abraham dropped his hatred for Sodom and his love for his mission. He was ready to sacrifice his life and have his new Torah appear to be a total failure. He was prepared to forgo his hopes and his vision for the future just so that Sodom would not be destroyed. This is *hesed* in the full sense of the word.

I Am Dust and Ashes

Another fundamental idea of Judaism that was developed by Abraham and upon which many commandments are based is expressed in a remarkable statement in Abraham's plea for

Sodom: "Abraham answered and said: I am aware that I have just begun to speak to God, and that I am dust and ashes" (Gen. 18:27). A person who can stand in the presence of the infinite God and, so to speak, argue with Him must feel mightily important. Yet the same person is fully aware that he is but dust and ashes, nothing whatsoever. This phrase has become a foundation of our worldview. The Halakhah built the laws of modesty on the dichotomy of importance and worthlessness.

On the one hand, modesty derives from "I am aware that I have just begun to speak to God," the consciousness of man's importance due to his perpetual standing in the presence of the Infinite: "And Abraham still stood before the Lord" (Gen. 18:22). Rema comments on the verse "I place God before me always" (Ps. 16:8):

> This is an important theme of the Torah. . . . A person's actions and interactions when he is alone are not the same as his actions and interactions when he stands before a great king, and he does not speak before a king as he would when by himself. If that is the case, how much more so [must a man watch himself] if he realizes he is in the presence of the one and only God, blessed be He, whose glory fills all the world and who watches and sees all men's actions (*Shulhan Arukh, Orah Hayyim* 1:1).

We must never forget God's constant presence, and this knowledge will always give us worth and importance. The infinite God is man's companion.

When Judaism speaks of man's importance, it does not ground this importance only in man's intellect or his spirit, as the Greeks did. The human body is even more important to Judaism. Every organ is holy; every member of the body has an important function; every physiological function is important. We have to respect our bodies, their impulses and their func-

tions. Our body must be clean and holy; we must not defile ourselves by lowering our bodies to the level of an animal's body. If
God is willing to walk with a human being, that person must
feel that his body and soul are important. The laws of modesty
are the antithesis of "I am dust and ashes," the notion that an
individual is worthless.

Respect for our body is expressed in laws pertaining to the
most intimate parts of human life. We must not mistreat our
bodies, even in the bedroom or the bath. The concept of modesty
is based on human worth, on the basis of Abraham's opening
statement, "I am aware that I have just begun to speak to God."
On this thesis are dependent the laws of respect for others, the
burying of the dead, the laws of mourning, of visiting the sick,
and so on. Modesty also encompasses the sanctity of sexual life.
There is no other area in which a person can sin so abysmally
as in the area of sexuality. He can transform himself into an animal. Judaism is very stringent about forbidden sexual relationships. Indeed, the sanctity of the Jewish family is based on the
laws of forbidden sexual relations.

On the other hand, modesty is also based on the principle of
"I am dust and ashes." Forgetting this principle can undermine
the basis of sanctity and morality. How did it come about that
the word *tzeni'ut*, which means modesty and humility, was
transformed into a term referring to sexual morality? It is
because immorality of all kinds stems from the pride of those
who love themselves and glorify themselves, those who believe
that they are central figures, that whatever pleases them and
whatever they want to do is permissible. "And the sons of God
saw that the daughters of man were good, and they took for
themselves wives as they chose" (Gen. 6:2). At that point, the
commandment "You shall not covet" (Ex. 20:13, Deut. 5:17)
became critical, and transgressing it led to thievery, murder,
and prostitution. Judaism most certainly believes in the worth
of the individual. It was the first religion to proclaim to the
world the idea of man's being made in the image of God, and it

formulated the maxim "He who destroys one person, it is as if he destroyed an entire world" (Mishnah *Sanhedrin* 4:5, according to the text of Maimonides and others). However, Judaism also requires us to understand that the same importance accorded to us must be accorded to others. The next person is also a unique individual; he too was created in God's image. And that is why we must not glorify ourselves at the expense of others. "What makes you think your blood is redder than your neighbor's? Perhaps his blood is redder than yours?" (*Sanhedrin* 74a).

All of the laws of damages are built on this principle. Those who learn *Bava Batra* understand how careful we must be to not do anything that can harm our neighbor. Modesty means that we must not insist that we can do what we want on our own property. "One must keep away the tar, the garbage, and the salt from one's neighbor's wall" (Mishnah *Bava Batra* 2:1), and "one must keep the pigeon hutch at a distance of fifty cubits from the city limits" because the pigeons might fill up the neighbors' gardens (Mishnah *Bava Batra* 2:5). In short, "A man should be more heedful of not doing harm to others than of not having harm done to himself" (Tosafot, *Bava Kamma* 23a, s.v. *ve-lihayav*).

The Torah teaches that the individual is important, but that his friend is just as important. Judaism contended that a person who show temerity, who is egotistical, and thus harms others, loses thereby his God-like image. The Mishnah in *Bava Kamma* (1:1) lists four major sources of damage: the ox, the ditch, the "*mav'eh*," and fire. In the Gemara (3b) there is substantial discussion on the category of the *mav'eh*. Rav says the "*mav'eh*" is damage done by a human being. However, if the *mav'eh* refers to damage caused by a person, why didn't Rebbi, the author of the Mishnah, simply say: "These are the four sources of damage: the ox, the ditch, man, and fire?" Why did he use a term that his students would not understand? The answer is that a person who does harm stops being a person. He is transformed into a creature called "*mav'eh*," a mere destroyer. It is not for nothing that the laws of damages appear in the Torah immediately after the account of the giving of the Torah (in *Parashat Mishpatim*). The Torah forbade slander and gossip for the same reason. We each have to remember that we are not the only ones who want to be treated decently by others. Hillel put it very nicely: "What is hated by you, do not do to your fellow" (*Shabbat* 31a). The individual is very important, but everyone has this importance. Sometimes the individual must say, "I am dust and ashes."

Modesty and the message of "I am dust and ashes" are even more apparent in another area. Anyone who has studied our history will be familiar with this striking phenomenon. In the case of other nations, we have accounts of the lives of great figures with many biographical details. For example, Aristotle, Plato, and Socrates, who lived more than twenty-four hundred years ago, are well known to us. We know their works and are fairly well informed about their private lives. We even know what the eighteenth-century wise men of other nations ate and what wine they drank.

However—and this demonstrates the great divide between us and others—we have very little biographical information about our great men. I am not talking only about those who lived thousands of years ago, like the prophet Isaiah, Ezekiel ben Buzi the priest, Rabban Yohanan ben Zakai, or Rabbi Yehoshua ben Hananya, but even about the great men who lived in the eighteenth century, like the Gaon of Vilna and Reb Hayyim of Volozhin. The little we know about them is known to us only by accident; for example, a chance fact in one of their responsa that casts some light on their private life. They appear to us anonymously, like mute figures, without a name or a time frame. Who were the men of the Great Assembly who saved our people from disappearing? Our sages tell us that 120 sages established the Great Assembly, but we know only a few names: Ezra, Nehemiah, Shimon the Righteous. Who were the members of Beit Shammai and Beit Hillel? Who were the *hasidim rishonim*? Who were the *soferim* or the sons of prophets, who, so say our sages, numbered in the thousands? The Mishnah says that by right no names should have been mentioned, and the opinions it records should all have been anonymous (*Eduyot* 1:4–5). Giving the names of individuals was permitted, however, for a practical reason. "R. Yehudah says: Why do we mention the name of an individual whose opinion differs from that of the majority? So that we may counteract the majority opinion; and if someone were to come and say 'I accept it' [the minority opinion], then all can say to him: 'Your tradition is like that minority opinion' " (*Eduyot* 1:6–7). If not for this generalization, we would not know any of our rabbis by name.

This striking concept expresses the unnatural modesty of the great men of our nation and of its sages. Individualism plays no role at all. No doubt every sage is important, but there are thousands of others equally important. The individual sage's importance stems only from the fact that his life was devoted to the great idea of the eternity of the Jewish people as manifested in the oral law. What is important in any case is his contribution to this eternity—his statements, his laws, his amendments, his worldviews. All these things were registered in the Torah; his private life is of no interest.

The great men of our nation were shy; they did not seek to put their private lives before the public. Even with regard to the greatest of them, the Torah tells us only as much as had some impact on the founding of the Jewish people and on their role as emissaries of the divine plan. Moses spent fifty or sixty years in Midian, and we do not know even one fact about him during this time.

The great idea of the Jewish community, namely, the binding of oneself to the Creator of the world, hovers around our sages. However, they are modest and seek no glory. "And I am dust and ashes."

Saving Lot's Daughters

The angels left Abraham and went to Sodom to destroy the city and save Lot and his family. To understand their mission, let us read a very strange and puzzling talmudic passage:

> Rava said: What is the meaning of the verse "Then said I: Lo, I am come with the scroll of a book which is prescribed for me" (Ps. 40:8)? David said [when he became king], "I thought that I have come only now, but I did not know that in the scroll of the book it was already written about me. For there (Gen. 19:15) it is written, '[The angels hastened Lot, saying: Take your wife and your two daughters] who can be found, *ha-nimtza'ot*,' and here (Ps. 89:21) it is written, 'I have found, *matzati*, David My servant; with My sacred oil I have anointed him' " (*Yevamot* 77a).

David thought that he had just entered Jewish history, that he had entered our annals and become a historical figure when the prophet Samuel anointed him with holy oil. He did not know that the Almighty had been concerned about him centuries earlier when He saved Lot and the angels told him, "Take your wife and your two daughters who can be found."

Why were the angels so concerned about Lot's two daughters? Why did they specifically tell Lot to take the girls out of the city because of its impending destruction? The reason is that Lot's daughters were the ancestors of the Messiah. Ruth, a descendant of Moab, was the mother of the Davidic dynasty (Ruth 4:17). Naamah the Ammonitess was the mother of Rehoboam (I Kings 14:21), and the King Messiah will be a descendant of David, Solomon, and Rehoboam. God did not send the angels because He was interested in Lot or in his daughters. He was interested in something else—the Messiah. The great vision of a redeemed world would have been made impossible if Lot's daughters had been destroyed in Sodom. That is why the

Torah is so interested in telling us the strange story of the act of incest that took place in the cave. Why else would the Torah record such an ugly event? It is not a story of incest. It is the story of the Messiah.

The personality of the King Messiah is not monotonic. God weaves the personality of the Messiah with vast amounts of multicolored threads, like Joseph's shirt. The messianic soul is iridescent, multi-talented, rich in thought-filled volition, and will be endowed with talents that seem mutually exclusive. But everything good and fine and noble in man must be passed on to the Messiah. He will have the capacity for *gevurah* and *hesed*. He will be a hero with unlimited power and strength who will defend justice. He will also be a man of unlimited loving-kindness, humble and simple. All these capabilities, capacities, and talents will merge in beautiful harmony in the King Messiah. The Messiah will represent creation at its best. Apparently, then, Lot's daughters had something beautiful in them to contribute to the Messiah's rich and powerful personality. If there is something fine in the non-Jewish families of the earth, it, too, will be passed on to the Messiah.

> R. Eleazar stated: What is meant by the verse "And in you shall the families of the earth be blessed, *ve-nivrekhu vekha*" (Gen. 12:3)? The Holy One, blessed be He, said to Abraham, "I have two goodly shoots to engraft on to you, *lehavrikh bakh*: Ruth the Moabitess and Naamah the Ammonitess" (*Yevamot* 63a).

Lot's daughter had something beautiful to contribute to the emerging personality of the King Messiah. What did this primitive girl possess that the Almighty, gathering virtues and noble traits from all over the world, picked up? She was uncouth and primitive, she committed incest, and yet she was the great-great-grandmother of Ruth. The Messiah will be her descendant!

She was under the impression, says Rashi (Gen. 19:31), that a cosmic cataclysm had struck and only three human beings had survived. (Years ago, we were unable to imagine this, but now we understand that it is something that can happen any day.) She acted as she did because she wanted to save humanity. This girl wanted to rebuild the world, to start from scratch and raise another race to take the place of the human race, which she believed had been destroyed simultaneously with the destruction of Sodom. This was heroism of an undreamt caliber. Instead of giving up, she had the courage to try to rebuild the world, to make a new humanity arise from the ashes of Sodom. She convinced her younger sister. Never mind that their method was primitive and crude. These two girls took upon themselves an impossible task, something staggering and awesome.

"And the firstborn said unto the younger: Our father is old and there is not a man in earth. . . . Come, let us make our father drink wine, that we may preserve the seed of our father" (Gen. 19:31–32). The plan *per se* was reprehensible, but their motivation was imaginative, noble, and heroic. The King Messiah will save the world. Indeed, he will achieve what his great-great-grandmothers wanted to do. The great-great-grandson, the King Messiah, will accomplish what the lonely girls could not. The heroism of Lot's daughters consisted in their commitment to mankind and their urge to save it.

The Messiah has another grandmother who came to us from the gentile world: Tamar, the daughter-in-law of Judah. She was the great-great-grandmother of Boaz and consequently of David and therefore of the King Messiah. The Torah tells us, "It came to pass at that time that Judah went down from his brethren . . . and saw there the daughter of a certain Canaanite" (Gen. 38:1). The Midrash says that "at that time" means that everyone was busy: Jacob was busy mourning Joseph, Joseph was busy mourning his fate, Reuben was busy mourning his lost opportunity, Judah was busy choosing a wife, and "God was busy creating the light of the King Messiah" (Gen. Rabbah

85:1). In other words, Judah set in motion a process leading to his ultimate marriage to Tamar, which resulted in the inspired personality of the Messiah.

Tamar was a heroic woman, a great woman. God gleaned and gathered beautiful things from throughout the world—gems, noble emotions, heroic capabilities. What could Tamar do that others could not? She could wait; she possessed the heroic ability and patience to wait without end.

> Judah told Tamar, his daughter-in-law, "Remain a widow in your father's house until Shelah my son be grown up," for he said [to himself], "Lest he also die like his brothers." Tamar went and dwelt in her father's house. And in process of time, Shua's daughter, the wife of Judah, died . . . (Gen. 38:11–12).

Tamar waited many years. She was lonely, forsaken, forgotten by everyone. Seasons passed. All her friends married, reared families; all contact with them came to an end; people treated her with ridicule and contempt. Shelah married; Judah had forgotten her. And yet she waited and never said a word. Wasn't she the incarnation of *Keneset Yisrael*, which has waited for her Beloved hundreds and thousands of years under the most trying circumstances? Did not Tamar personify the greatest of all heroic action—to wait while the waiting arouses laughter and derision?

The Messiah has yet another grandmother who came to us from the gentile world—Ruth. She, too, was heroic. Boaz acknowledged the great courage of this pagan girl in casting her lot with a people she did not previously know.

> Boaz answered and said to her: "It has fully been told me all that you have done unto your mother-in law since the death of your husband, and how you have left your father and your mother and the land of your nativity and

> are come into a people that you knew not heretofore.
> May the Lord recompense your work, and may your
> reward be complete from the Lord, the God of Israel,
> under whose wings you have come to take refuge" (Ruth
> 2:11).

When we read these words thanking Ruth for joining a people which she knew not, we willy-nilly think of the question that is addressed to any non-Jew who applies for *gerut*: "What prompts you to convert? Do you not know that the Jews at this time are persecuted and oppressed, despised, harassed and overcome by afflictions?" (*Yevamot* 47a). Of course, Boaz did not say it explicitly; but the meaning of his words points toward the same truth: only a hero joins our strange and lonely people.

It is amazing! The words of Boaz were spoken at the dawn of Jewish history, at a time when the tension between Jew and non-Jew was as yet unknown. This episode preceded Haman's hatred and indictment of the Jews, the Alexandrian hate literature, and the Gospels. The world knew nothing of the Jew's uniqueness, his so-called isolationism and egocentrism. Nevertheless, Boaz admired Ruth's fortitude for daring to join a strange and misunderstood people.

We Jews have been a strange people since the very birth of our nation. It has always taken courage, the ability to do something bold, to defy public resentment and identify with this unknown, mysterious people. What was mysterious about the Jews in early biblical times? The mere fact that they were not pagans, that they believed in one invisible and incorporeal God, was puzzling to pagans. Moreover, the Jews served their God by preaching morality, whereas the pagans worshipped their idols by giving gifts to them, by intoxicating themselves with orgiastic pleasure, by living like voluptuaries.

Ruth was a heroic woman; she joined a people alien to her, and committed herself to a way of life she did not understand. She came from a pagan background, where unlimited pleasure and over-indulgence were an element in worship, and she joined a religion that demands discipline, redemption of the biological call for gratification.

To outsiders, Judaism is a difficult religion. The mere fact that the Halakhah interferes with every phase of human life, that Judaism is so concerned with the trivial, makes the commitment seem staggering and almost superhuman. To convert to Judaism and accept an all-inclusive Judaic commitment borders on the heroic. In addition, even as early as the period of the Judges, to become a Jew has meant to be alienated from the rest of the world. The destiny of *Avraham ha-Ivri*, the lonely Abraham, has always accompanied the Jews.

In a word, *gerut* is heroic action at the level of observance and practical living, and also at the level of one's relationship with the non-Jewish world. No wonder the Talmud says that the Jews, upon responding "We shall do and obey," were called *gibborei koah*, heroes (*Shabbat* 88a).

The King Messiah must be endowed with heroic qualities, for he is coming to change the status quo, to revolutionize concepts and opinions, to transform our outlook on life. He will defy evil, oppose ruthlessness, challenge injustice, "and decide with equity for the meek of the earth; and he shall smite the land with the rod of his mouth and with the breath of his lips shall he slay the wicked" (Isa. 11:4). Messianism minus heroic action is meaningless.

The poor of biblical times used to glean and gather after the reapers. The Almighty, too, gleaned and gathered—not ears of corn but beautiful inclinations and noble virtues. From them He wove the soul of the King Messiah. God found a heroic girl in Moab. The Almighty was "busy" with the formation and creation of the Messiah's personality, which was to embody the finest and most beautiful elements concealed in the depths of mankind. God brought the girl to Judea so that she could collaborate with Him in creating a Messiah personality. She contributed the heroism of loneliness and acceptance of the incomprehensible.

Ruth, no matter how idealistic she was, no matter how sturdy her character, no matter how heroic and revolutionary her spirit, was in her heart deeply loyal and grateful. In fact, her heroism was the consequence of her loyalty to her mother-in-law. Her first words, "Do not entreat me to leave you" (Ruth 1:16), tell a story of great humility. She revered her mother-in-law. When Naomi told her to do something odd, namely, to visit the threshing floor and uncover Boaz's feet, she did not argue with her mother-in-law. "And she did according to all that her mother-in-law bade her" (Ruth 3:6). Respect for the elderly, humility, and a sense of gratitude are indispensable. Heroism is important, provided it goes hand in hand with humility and loyalty.

The Jewish people have not given up the dream of reforming, changing, and transforming humanity. The *Malkhuyot* section of the Rosh Ha-Shanah *Amidah* is devoted exclusively to our idea and vision that someday, no matter how distant it may be, we will achieve our objective. This is the idea of the Messiah. We are interested in the coming of the Messiah not only as Jews but also as human beings, to save the world, to wipe out evil.

The Torah was not given to non-Jews directly, but the Almighty has offered it to all of mankind indirectly, as a promise, a vision, an eschatological expectation, the ultimate end of history. The Torah was given to us so many millennia ago. Our task was and still is to teach the Torah to mankind, to influence the non-Jewish world, to redeem it from an orgiastic way of living, from cruelty and insensitivity, to arouse in mankind a sense of justice and fairness. In a word, we are to teach the world the seven *mitzvot* that are binding on every human being.

But we have also been assigned another mission: to be the message carrier and mentor not only of the seven *mitzvot* that apply to the descendants of Noah, that is, to the human race as a whole, but also of a total outlook on life, the entire moral system to which Jews are committed. The non-Jewish world is expected to take note of the Torah life we lead, to admire our ways, our customs and mores, our *mishpatim* and *hukkim,* both our rational and non-rational commandments. The Jews must stand out in society as exemplars; our way of life must impress and attract people and fascinate their curiosity. The Jew must always bear witness to his peculiar relationship with God.

> Behold, I have taught you statutes and judgments, even as the Lord my God commanded me, that you should act accordingly in the land whither you go to possess. Observe therefore and do them; for this is your wisdom and your understanding in the sight of the peoples, that, when they hear all these statutes, shall say: "Surely this great nation is a wise and understanding people" (Deut. 4:5–6).

This principle underlies the commandment of *kiddush ha-Shem*, sanctification of the Divine Name, and the prohibition of *hillul ha-Shem*, desecration of the Divine Name.

Mattan Torah, the giving of the Torah, initiated the messianic process of redeeming the world from its crudity and profanity. The Torah was given to the Jew, who was told to disseminate the word of God among pagans, atheists, agnostics, and hedonists, thereby bringing them to their Maker. It is a piecemeal, slow movement. Nevertheless, it will be consummated in the messianic era, when "the mountain of the Lord's house shall be established on the top of the mountains" (Isa. 2:2).

Mattan Torah is bound up with the Messiah, who will possess the heroism of his grandmothers whom the Almighty found in the non-Jewish world. They represented the heroism of loneliness, the heroism of universal commitment, and the heroism of faith and waiting. The ideal of *mattan Torah* will be fully realized only in the time of the Messiah. This great vision of a redeemed world would have been impossible had Lot's daughters been destroyed in Sodom.

❧ *From Generation to Generation*

Young and Old

Abraham survived Sarah by thirty-eight years. But the Torah says very little about his activities following Sarah's death. Only two events are recorded, the purchase of a grave for Sarah and the marrying off of Isaac. The second story is told not so much to portray Abraham, but to acquaint us with the second mother of the covenantal community, Rebecca, who succeeded Sarah. The vacuum created by Sarah's death was filled (Gen. 24:67). Now the covenant can be continued, because there is a mother in the covenantal community—not only a father but a mother as well. The Torah tells us nothing else about Abraham because the covenant was entrusted to two, a man and a woman; if the latter is missing, the story of the covenantal community comes to a temporary halt.

The Torah tells us that "The life of Sarah was a hundred years and twenty years and seven years; these were the years of Sarah's life" (Gen. 23:1). Rashi, based on the Midrash (Gen. Rabbah 58:1), comments:

The word *shanah* ("years") was written after every item to tell us that each term is interpreted individually. At one hundred she was like twenty as regards sin; just as a twenty-year-old girl is considered not to have sinned, since she is not liable to punishment, so was Sarah at one hundred without sin. And at twenty Sarah was, as regards beauty, like a girl of seven. "These were the years of Sarah's life"—they were all replete with goodness.

There is another text:

At one hundred she was as beautiful as a girl of twenty; at twenty she was, as regards sin, as innocent as a child of seven (*Yalkut Shim'oni*, Psalms, 730).

In my opinion, the second text is superior to the first. In relation to sin, the equation of seven and twenty is more apt than that of twenty and a hundred. The same goes for the comparison of one hundred with twenty as far as appearance is concerned.

The two texts embody two different concepts of liability for punishment. According to the first, the term is related to retribution by the heavenly court. That is why a girl before age twenty is not guilty of sin.

The text we have suggested speaks in terms of justice administered by the human court. As far as human justice is concerned, the age of responsibility begins not at twenty but at twelve. A girl of seven is morally not responsible; the very instant she turns twelve, she becomes a responsible person and is punished for her transgressions.

However we organize these two equations (one hundred as twenty, and twenty as seven), the question of primary importance is: What is their meaning? *Shanah* signifies an entity, a time period, a stage or an era in the human life span. Hebrew grammar often uses the singular to describe a plural of more than ten. We say *ha-yom assara yamim* and *ha-yom ahad assar yom*. The plural expressed in the singular takes the many and unifies them into an entity. In the case of *shanah*, describing many years, the singular denotes an era, a period of time which represents not just a time unit but a unique existential experience. *Hayyim*, "life," is constructed as a plural. Sarah lived three lives: the life of a child, the life of a young woman, and the life of a mature and old woman.

Moreover, these time entities, or existential experiences, are not arranged in a vertical, mutually exclusive order of succession, as is commonly accepted. We think that one starts with being a child, and when the childhood period passes, the individual enters another domain, namely that of youth. When one leaves youth, he finds himself in the embrace of maturity, followed by old age. In a word, the experiences of childhood, youth, and maturity do not coexist; they follow each other. The end of one signals the emergence of the next.

In the realm of chemical processes, there is no way to retain biological youth in a middle-aged person, nor can the pattern of the middle-aged be preserved in old age. The sequence is strict and unalterable in the development of what we call organic existence, or life. In the realm of the unfolding of the spirit, however, it is possible to see youth and ripe age—or even childhood and youth—as simultaneous experiences. The advanced in years quite often display spiritual restlessness and intensity, and the young are sometimes characterized by cautious wisdom and sober judgment. An old person may be wonderfully childlike with a dreamer's naiveté and excitement. The idealism of youth quite often shines through the eyes of the graybeard. In fact, great people are sometimes great children. They are rich and multitalented because of their age; they are beautiful too because of their honesty and sincerity. Sarah was at one and the same time seven, twenty, and a hundred years old. She was simultaneously very old and very young, representing the aged, the adult, and the child.

"These are the *lives* of Sarah": she was always a one-hundred-year-old mature person, a twenty-year-old girl, and a seven-year-old child.

J. M. Barrie's Peter Pan was a boy who refused to grow up and assume responsibility. However, Sarah at twenty was mature and fully developed both intellectually and emotionally; she was energetic, bold, and daring. Yet the adult in Sarah did not destroy the child. Maturity did not do away with childhood. In the deep recesses of her personality, no matter how developed, no matter how capable and brilliant, no matter how attractive and ingenious, always resided an innocent child. The adult might have reached the highest peak of intellectual greatness or growth, her creative cultural activities might have been enormous, yet all that did not interfere with the secret presence of a child in Sarah. Notwithstanding the maturation of her natural wisdom, she retained within her the young girl she had been once upon a time. She acted like a mature, wise, experience-rich old woman, but in times of need and crisis the young, bold, courageous girl came to the fore and took over.

Abraham, like Sarah, was a child all his life. Abraham was extremely inquisitive; every star twinkling in the Mesopotamian heavens mystified him; every flower in the field and every drop of dew puzzled him. His curiosity made him restless; he explored the universe. He quite often failed to find an answer to his questions; he experimented time and again until the great mystery was revealed.

Youth represents idealism. The young are committed unconditionally. They arrogantly defy the world. Abraham, like Sarah, was a youth all his life; he defied the society of which he was a part. He shattered the idols as an act of holy arrogance. He dared to be an iconoclast in a pagan society that worshipped icons.

The ability to be all three together, to experience existentially child, youth, and old age, is a sign of the covenantal community. Let me explain this in semi-halakhic terms. There are three *mitzvot* that play a central role in our religious life: *talmud Torah*, prayer, and *emunah*, faith. *Talmud Torah* is more or less an esoteric gesture. As with all intellectual and scientific gestures, the more capable one is, and the more time one can afford to spend on the study of Torah, the more scholarship one accumulates. The *zaken*, the old person, is the wise person, because he has had more opportunities and more hours to spend in the tent of Torah. That is why we equate *zaken* with *hakham,* age with wisdom. Maturity is important for the study of Torah; an immature mind cannot study, cannot grasp, cannot abstract, cannot analyze, cannot infer. The mature mind is capable of accomplishing miracles. God wants man to grow intellectually, to expand his capacity for analyzing, comparing, conceptualizing, and inferring. As far as *talmud Torah* is concerned, the grown-up, the adult, the trained mind, is the ideal person.

However, we may suddenly find ourselves holding the *siddur*, the prayer book, instead of the Gemara. Prayer is an art, not just a mechanical performance. It is an attitude, a state of mind, a mood. It is a great and exciting experience, an adventure. But when we find ourselves holding the prayer book, when we are about to recite our prayers and pour out our hearts before God, the scene changes completely. The adult, the proud mind, the independent thinker, the genius—none of them are admitted to the *heikhal ha-tefillah*, the palace of prayer. They do not know the art of prayer. *Talmud Torah* requires self-affirmation and self-appreciation, confidence in one's ability to understand and judge, to discriminate and equate. *Tefillah* demands self-negation, just the opposite approach. The mood that generates a desire for prayer is one of hopelessness and bankruptcy. To pray means to surrender one's pride and self-confidence, to put aside any awareness of greatness, freedom, and independence. Prayer is for those who are simple, who are capable of complete surrender and of complete trust in the Holy One, "whose heart is not haughty . . . whose soul is like that of a weaned child" (Ps. 131:1–2). Instinctively, the child feels that he is in the embrace of someone who loves him very much, who will protect him and do anything to make his life happy and better. That feeling is the very root of prayer.

There is another very important religious act which only the child in a person can perform. This is *emunah*. The English word "faith," like many other words, is profaned when applied as a mindset concerning people. "I have faith in him," we say. From a strictly philosophical and theological viewpoint, no one can have faith in man. Indeed, it is blasphemy to have faith in man. Faith means complete trust, that the person in whom I have faith will never betray me. To say I have faith in man means to contradict David's statement that "Every man is a liar" (Ps. 116:11). One cannot have absolute faith in a liar.

Faith in God requires of the faithful suspension of judgment or suspension of the logos, surrender not only of the body but also of the mind. *Emunah* sometimes confronts us with a challenge to suspend our judgment, to act irrationally, to act illogically, to act even though we do not understand why we are acting in a certain way.

This is what was required of Abraham. He undoubtedly was teaching everyone who cared to learn and to listen that murder is a heinous crime, that human sacrifices are abominable. He was engaged in an inexorable struggle with the pagan priests. He used to build altars, but he never sacrificed anything on them—with the exception of the last altar he built, on Mount Moriah, on which he sacrificed the ram as a substitute for Isaac.

Suddenly this same Abraham received a call to perform a human sacrifice! Abraham could have asked immediately: My Master, You appointed me as Your apostle, Your representative, to teach people how to worship God, how to practice morality and hate cruelty. For many years I have been fighting pagan practices, for many years I have been preaching and speaking against the ugly custom of killing young children on altars. Now you command me to do the same thing? What will the world say? How will I be able to explain it to myself? I have followed You since the time we had our first meeting somewhere in Ur of the Chaldees, I have never rebelled against You; but now You ask the impossible, that I should suspend my humanity.

However, we all know that Abraham did not say a single word; not a single complaint came forth from his mouth. Silently he accepted God's command, suspended his logical as well as his moral judgment, suspended his own humanity and was ready to do the very thing he hated most. An adult could not do that; only a child is capable of absolute, unconditional surrender to the point of giving up one's humanity, one's conscience.

That is exactly what God demands from us: suspension of judgment. But for us it is not as difficult as it was for Abraham. All God wants from us is to not rationalize the *mitzvot*, to not try to explain each and every mitzvah, saying, "This mitzvah makes sense, this other mitzvah doesn't." All we have to do is accept the Torah *in toto*. As a matter of fact, it is not suspension of judgment that is required, the way it was with Abraham. Our minds are limited, our rational capacity restricted. We are frail beings, we are ignorant; the fact that our intellect does not digest some *hukkim* does not mean that God wants us to suspend our judgment. A sense of modesty suffices.

Abraham was an intellectual giant, a genius of frightening stature. His judgment was mature and ripe. He was not a child, and yet he was capable of transforming himself into a child and accepting the Almighty's command to suspend his judgment and his humanity, to do something inhuman.

This great Abraham, the Knight of Faith, as Kierkegaard calls him in *Fear and Trembling*, was the first to pray and the first to have faith in God. Both require just one transformation, one metamorphosis, namely, from adult into child. Abraham, whose glance boldly penetrated the starlit heavens of Mesopotamia, who courageously revolutionized human thought, turned into a small child when he was about to pray or to perform the act of faith.

Talmud Torah requires adulthood; prayer and faith require childhood. We must be ready for both; we must be capable of assuming the identity either of a child or of an adult. The Talmud says, "The coin issued by Abraham had the images of an old man and woman on one side, and the images of a young boy and girl on the other side" (*Bava Kamma* 97b). Sarah and Abraham merged together; they were old and young at the same time.

Sarah's young-old personality is manifest in the birth of Isaac. No one expected so extraordinary an event to take place, and she reacted in a dual way. First she laughed; she was overwhelmed with joy. She kept on repeating: Who would have believed that I was capable of bearing children! Her question revolved about her companions, who teased and ridiculed her.

However, Sarah well understood that God was not granting her a child for social reasons. She knew that something greater and more important would happen because of this strange birth. She shivered, standing in awe and ecstasy before this incomprehensible and frightening event. She was aware of the awesome responsibility which was thereby imposed upon her, to be the mother of nations. "For the son of this bondwoman shall not be heir with my son" (Gen. 21:10).

On the one hand, Sarah laughed; on the other hand, she was frightened by the responsibility of a covenantal community that was entrusted to her. Sarah was both child and old woman, a hundred years old and seven years old. When individuals are happy and give thanks to God, they must express their gratitude on many levels. They are obligated to thank God as adults, as mature individuals. The medium of manifestation will consist in understanding and profoundly appreciating the kindness and *hesed* the Almighty has bestowed upon them, and the accompanying great responsibility. The joy is quiet and seems restrained. However, one must also thank God in a childlike manner, in the vocabulary of a youngster whose feelings are not subdued. Even the greatest must not hide their excitement, their wonderful state of mind. They should rejoice aloud as if they were children.

Michal was critical of her husband King David's undisciplined behavior on the occasion of bringing the ark to Jerusalem. He was happy, and like a child he displayed his happiness. "King David was dancing and jumping with all his might" (II Sam. 6:14). At that moment King David was again a lad! *Simhat beit ha-sho'evah* consisted in merrymaking and rejoicing by *gedolei Yisrael* in a way reminiscent of David. The most prominent of them engaged in singing, playing musical instruments, acrobatics, and entertaining the ordinary people who came to watch the wonderful celebration. Maimonides writes that only the most outstanding scholars performed at these celebrations (*Hilkhot Lulav* 8:14). It was necessary for them to put on a show for the pilgrims and the citizens of Jerusalem. The *simhat beit ha-sho'evah* required them to behave and rejoice not like learned grown-ups but like excited children. God loves children. "Is Ephraim my dear son?" (Jer. 31:19). "When Israel was a child, then I loved him" (Hosea 11:1).

Abraham's life story, as told by the Torah, begins at the age of seventy-five and comes to an end with Sarah's death. The originator of the covenant and creator of a new moral code was not a single individual. Two people were charged with the task, a man and a woman, Abraham and Sarah. They were both indispensable for the implementation of the divine plan. Both of them converted people; both taught the many. Once Sarah died, Abraham's assignment came to an end. He was ordered by the Almighty to withdraw from the arena of history, retreat into privacy, and live like an ordinary person. The vacancy was filled by someone else who was instructed to step into history and live as the father of a nation, Isaac. Of course, the second assignment included a woman as well—Rebecca, who took the place of Sarah. The covenant had to have a father and a mother.

Eliezer's journey resulted in the discovery of Rebecca as the successor of Sarah.

Isaac and Rebecca

Until the *Akedah,* Abraham and Isaac were a team; there was no contradiction between what Abraham represented and what Isaac personified. Together they preached, taught, and tried to embody and inculcate *hesed.* Of course, Abraham was the patriarch of the covenantal community, Isaac the junior partner. Nevertheless they constituted a harmonious whole.

The *Akedah*, however, fashioned a new personality, a new soul, for Isaac, and a new covenantal reality. The unity of "they both went together" (Gen. 22:8) was lost. The two ideas that Abraham and Isaac respectively represented were not merged. Instead their activities began to contradict each other. Abraham symbolized *hesed*, an overflowing love that rises like a river in springtime and inundates its environs. Abraham wanted to convert all of mankind. He was concerned with the whole world. He sat by the highway waiting for travelers; he carried his morality to the people and wanted to proselytize everyone. Isaac symbolized *gevurah*, self-limitation and self-concentration, heroic action and withdrawal. With the *Akedah*, contradiction replaced peace, tension substituted for togetherness. "Abraham returned to his young men" (Gen. 22:19), but Isaac belonged to a world of his own. They now moved along two different paths. Isaac did not return to Beersheba; he traveled to another destination, burdened with another task. Ibn Ezra (Gen. 22:19) says that Isaac was in his own dominion—*ki hu bi-reshuto.*

Isaac is a cryptic figure. The Bible envelops him in a cloud of mystery and does not tell us much about his life. Only two episodes are recorded, his sojourn in Gerar (the site of the conflict about the wells) and his role in the confrontation between Jacob and Esau. Even in these narratives, Isaac appears to react rather than act. While the Bible dedicated almost three *parashiyyot* to Abraham and a few others to Jacob, it describes

Isaac in only one *sidrah*. The Kabbalists try to explain this by the method of mystical symbolism. Abraham represents *hesed*, and Jacob *tiferet*. Both of these are, to some extent, accessible and intelligible to man. When times are good, man is confronted with the beautiful and rational. He feels God's footsteps in the natural as well as the historical universe. At such times, even ordinary people see God. Abraham and Jacob distinguished themselves with their openness and simplicity. Isaac represents the aspect of *pahad* (strict justice; see Ramban to Gen. 31:42) and *gevurah* (sacrificial heroic life). God, under the aspect of *gevurah,* is revealed to those who encounter evil, suffer, and live in agony. Sometimes God contacts man while the distance is endless and God's glory is wrapped up in an impenetrable mystery. Isaac represents this aspect of revelation. That is why his life story is cryptic.

Isaac marries only at the age of forty. He was dedicated and consecrated to God as a burnt offering. He was not allowed to enjoy the company of another human being, to share with other people in the joys life offers. Marriage was in direct conflict with his consecration to God. Only after he was offered on the altar was he permitted to build a home.

Why did Abraham send Eliezer to select a mate for Isaac? Why didn't he choose a bride right there in the land of Canaan? Let us assume that he could not marry off Isaac to the daughter of a Canaanite because of the Almighty's promise pertaining to the land. Nevertheless, he was free to find a girl of another race. Our Sages say that Eliezer offered his daughter as a wife for Isaac, but Abraham refused (Gen. Rabbah 59:9).

Abraham had a sharp mind and was a critical observer. He had a sensitive soul, profound intuition, and was courageous, dignified, and imaginative. Because of these traits, God chose and appointed him as the father of the covenantal society. All the capabilities with which Abraham was blessed were inherited from his father and mother. Abraham was a human being and thus was subject to a family genetic code like any other being of flesh and blood. He thought that since the Almighty had chosen Nahor's family, there was something good in this family's code. That is why he sent Eliezer to Aram-Naharaim.

What key virtue did the members of this household possess that made them fit for and worthy of joining the covenant? The answer is *hesed*, kindness expressed through *hakhnasat orehim*, hospitality. Abraham distinguished himself in this mitzvah. *Hakhnasat orehim* is unique in embodying not only *hesed* but patience, too. Other acts of charity are indicative of a good, sympathetic soul who shares in the suffering and pain of a fellow human being. Hospitality, however, requires patience and perseverance. This virtue plays an important role; it constitutes a central virtue in the table of the thirteen attributes of mercy proclaimed by the Almighty to Moses in Sinai: God is *erekh appayim*, He waits for the sinner.

Hakhnasat orehim may have its source in one of two human qualities: either genuine kindness or civility and courtesy. A polite person quite often conveys the impression of being charitable and good, but inwardly he is completely indifferent and detached. The act of the polite person is related to an etiquette, the act of the kind person to an ethic.

The criterion that enables us to distinguish between politeness and kindness is quite obvious. The element of perseverance and patience is to be found in the kind person but not in the merely polite person. The kind person has unlimited patience. The needy may call on a kind person for help over a long period of time, for years and years. The appeal will always be heard and acted upon. The polite person's patience is limited. If repeatedly approached, he will stop extending help. Any illogical plea for help, any exaggeration or crossing the borderline of decency, will be harshly rejected and condemned if the helper is merely acting in accordance with etiquette. But in the case of kindness, there is no limit to the benefactor's perseverance and tolerance. He helps even people who are vulgar and coarse. He takes abuse. Nothing can alienate him from the person in need.

Eliezer wanted to find out what motivated Rebecca's actions. Was it spiritual nobility and kindness, or good manners and civility? He asked her to do things that were outrageous. He said, "Let me sip a little water from your pitcher" (Gen. 24:17), as opposed to asking her to hand him the pitcher. In other words, he told her that he would do nothing; she was to draw water from the well and pour it into his mouth. Isn't this distasteful and tactless? Had she just been polite, she would have splashed the water in his face. Why did he ask a young girl to water the camels, something women did not do in antiquity? Couldn't one of his servants have taken the pitcher down to the well, brought up the water, and taken care of the animals?

The answer is that Eliezer was testing her patience. She passed the test with flying colors. She did not feel hurt; she was not repulsed by the newcomer's primitive bluntness and lack of good manners. She practiced hospitality even though the traveler was coarse and rude. The quality of *erekh appayim* prevailed, and Rebecca became the mother of the nation.

There are three reasons for singling out *hakhnasat orehim* as the central virtue in Abraham's axiological hierarchy. First, hospitality is difficult and uncomfortable. We let a stranger into our house. His mannerisms are odd, his speech foreign. He eats differently, is crude and vulgar. His opinions are strange, and he intrudes upon our privacy. Abraham built altars (e.g., Gen. 12:7, 13:18). He sacrificed on the altars his comfort, his nobility, the happiness of an intimate private life with his beloved Sarah. He invited everyone to his tent, no matter how vulgar the guest was and how difficult to tolerate.

Second, the central experience in Abraham's life was *galut*—homelessness, wandering without knowing the destination, sleeping on the ground on freezing cold nights, being lost along the byways of a strange land. This passional experience taught Abraham and his descendants the art of involvement, of sharing in distress, of feeling for the stranger, of having compassion for the other. It trained Abraham to react quickly to suffering, to try to lighten the other's burden as much as possible. No matter who the stranger was, what he stood for, and how primitive he was, the stranger had suffered, and suffering purges a person and redeems him.

In general, the Torah ethic is derived from experience. We have mercy on all uprooted and defenseless human beings in exile. "You shall not wrong a stranger, neither shall you oppress him; for you were strangers in the land of Egypt" (Ex. 22:20). "The stranger that sojourns with you shall be unto you as the home-born among you, and you shall love him as yourself; for you were a stranger in the land of Egypt" (Lev. 19:34). We are burdened with an ethical norm to help because we remember how we felt when we were in distress.

This casts a light upon our mysterious historical destiny. Our nation was born in the crucible of exile, bondage, and suffering. We emerged as a people from the sand dunes of the Sinai Desert, where we wandered forty years. Why could we not rise as a people in our own land in prosperity and abundance? The answer is simple. If our morality had to be one of kindness and *hesed*, it could not have been formulated for people who knew not what suffering is. Only people in exile could understand and appreciate a morality of kindness. Therefore, *galut* was a central experience in the life of our patriarchs and it is still a major experience in our lives.

The third reason for the supremacy of the norm of hospitality is that the Torah resents and rejects the doctrine of "my home is my castle." This doctrine conveys two wrong ideas, two unfounded illusions: first, that the home gives us ample protection and shields us in times of crisis; second, that it is our property and no one else can claim a share in it. Both assertions are false. One is never fully protected; there is no total security. Man is exposed to all kinds of evil and disaster. He has neither a home nor a castle. He is not the lord; he is just a tenant and perhaps not even that. "For the land is Mine; for you are strangers and sojourners with Me" (Lev. 25:23).

The Almighty is the great *makhnis orehim*. His hospitality made it possible for humanity to exist, for the world to come into being. "To be" means to share in the infinite being of the Almighty. The Almighty, like Abraham, invites people to partake of His boundless existence. Creation is an act of *hakhnasat orehim*.

Our Sages (*Berakhot* 7b) said that Abraham was the first person to invoke God by the name *A-donai*. This name is of juridic origin; God owns the world in juridic terms. Not only does God run the cosmos *de facto*, but the cosmos is His *de jure*. We are just strangers whom the Almighty has invited into his "tent," which is the universe. How beautiful is the doctrine of *tzimtzum,* contraction. What is creation if not withdrawal by God in order to make it possible for a world to emerge in space and time? Infinity steps aside and finitude is born. What is *hakhnasat orehim* if not withdrawal by the master from a part of his home so that a stranger can occupy the empty part he vacates?

Rebecca was ready to join Abraham's community. When she came with Eliezer to Canaan and married Isaac, she did not act like a novice, a stranger who needed instruction and training in order to get acquainted with the ways of the new community. "Isaac brought her to his mother Sarah's tent, and took Rebecca, and she became his wife; and he loved her" (Gen. 24:67). Isaac brought her into the tent and she became exactly like his mother Sarah. She knew and practiced Abraham's moral code and way of life. Who taught her; who trained her to observe the basic principles of morality and piety?

The Torah tells us that "they sent away Rebecca their sister, and her nurse, and Abraham's servant, and his men" (Gen. 24:59). Why was it necessary to tell us that Rebecca's nurse joined the caravan? More intriguing is the verse "And Deborah, Rebecca's nurse, died, and she was buried beneath Beth-El under an oak; and the name of it was called Allon-Bakhut"

(Gen. 35:8). The Bible does not record the deaths of Rebecca and Leah, but it tells us about the death of Deborah.

The answer is plain. Deborah raised Rebecca. She made a great woman, a prophetess as holy as Sarah, from an ordinary pagan girl. Rebecca and her children listened to Deborah and let themselves be guided by her wisdom. Her death was a blow to Jacob and his family. Deborah, who brought up Rebecca, was a matriarch of the covenantal community. She was responsible for Rebecca's education and secret loyalty to Abraham's covenant. Deborah's pupil, the young Rebecca, displayed enormous strength of character when she proudly answered "I will go" (Gen. 24:58) to join Abraham's community.

Isaac Resembles Abraham

Rashi (Gen. 25:19) tells us that Isaac was made to bear a close resemblance to his father because cynics were circulating a rumor that Abraham was not his father. Hence the Almighty made Isaac's countenance in the image of Abraham.

It is interesting that Rashi (Gen. 21:7) speaks of similar malicious gossip against Abraham and Sarah. "Who would have said unto Abraham, Sarah should give children suck? For I have born him a son in his old age" (Gen. 21:7). The women brought their children along and Sarah fed all of them. The women gossiped that Sarah was not the child's mother, that she had found an abandoned baby and adopted it.

Two kinds of accusations were hurled: one that the baby was neither Sarah's nor Abraham's; the other that Sarah was the mother but Abraham was not the father. Why did the Torah take any cognizance of these ugly rumors fabricated by enemies? The Torah should have ignored them. One of the rumors, even though false, was at least not absurd; the other was sheer nonsense. The rumor that the child belonged to neither Sarah nor Abraham made some sense. Abraham and Sarah were too old to beget children. The second rumor was a plain absurdity for two reasons. First, a woman loses her capacity for conception much earlier in life than the male. Second, Abraham was capable of begetting a child, as shown by the fact that he had a son, Ishmael, with Hagar. It was Sarah who could not conceive.

When we read Abraham's life story, we get the impression that he was respected by his acquaintances and neighbors. We read about the Hittites and the purchase of the Cave of Machpelah (Gen. 23). They addressed Abraham with great respect and reverence. Abimelech, recognizing that Abraham was no ordinary man, asked him to sign a non-aggression treaty (Gen. 21:22-32). We don't come across any manifestations of disrespect or hostility. If so, why was such ugly gossip circulated about the birth of Isaac?

People did not object to Abraham's world outlook, to his unique way of life, to his moral code. On the contrary, they stood in awe of him. But that was only so long as they were convinced that it all would die with Abraham, that he had no spiritual heir and there would be no successor to continue the tradition. However, once Isaac was born they began to change their attitude. Abraham's way of life was not just an old man's idea; it has dynamism, life, aggressiveness. They knew that young Isaac would pick up the tradition and carry it on, and they resented this prospect; they wanted no spiritual succession. They began to spread rumors.

The rumors represented two philosophies. The first was that Judaism was obsolete, old-fashioned, and unfit as a guide for the modern world. At the beginning of the twentieth century, Jewish socialism took this stand vis-à-vis our faith. There are even now many people who reject religious Judaism *in toto*. Neither ritual and ceremonial nor morality is acceptable in our scientific philosophy, they say. They reject Abraham and Sarah. They maintain that history will finally dispose of all tradition.

Thanks to the general mood of contemporary man, afflicted by a sense of the emptiness and dreariness of a godless world, many secular Jews are now revising their philosophy. They do not reject Judaism completely. They try to discriminate between the ethos and the ritual, between law and ceremonial. They say that the beautiful and tender in Judaism, represented by Sarah, should be accepted and retained. Lovely Sarah belongs in the modern world. Ceremonialism and ideal morality are in keeping with the needs of modern life. However, they say, punctilious Abraham, who obeys commands and is guided by inflexible laws, is not qualified to teach modern man how to serve God. In truth, the traditions of both Sarah and Abraham are vital to Judaism, and Isaac was committed to the whole of Judaism.

Covenantal History

The Sinaitic covenant pertains only to human deed and action; it charts a way of doing things in every area of human endeavor. In contradistinction, the patriarchal covenant addresses itself not to human deeds but to the human personality as a whole, to the fundamental traits of human character, to the essence of our consciousness—I would prefer our "I consciousness." The patriarchal covenant is an existential covenant; it blazed a trail in the jungle of the human I-awareness and tried to tell man who he is, or rather who he should be. It told man how to experience his own reality, and how to be conscious of himself as a human being and a member of the covenantal community. In other words, the Sinaitic covenant tells the Jew what to do and how to act as a member of the covenantal community. The patriarchic covenant teaches the Jew how to feel as a member of that community and how to experience being a Jew. It is a great experience, but not everyone knows how to experience his Jewishness.

What is the covenantal personality fashioned by the patriarchs and matriarchs, by Sarah and Abraham, by Isaac and Rebecca, by Jacob, Rachel, and Leah? What kind of a personality was it? The basic characteristic of covenantal man and woman is the existential dialectic with which they are burdened, an awareness of greatness as well as of helplessness.

The patriarchal covenant created not only a covenantal personality but also a covenantal historical destiny. Covenantal history differs from other historical processes. The main distinction between universal and covenantal historical events lies in their different dynamics. Historical dynamics, at a universal level, is etiological. Every event is brought about by a cause.

The covenantal event, in my opinion, should be placed in a different causal context, namely teleology, purposiveness. The covenantal dynamic is sustained by the covenantal promise, by a goal that lies temporarily outside the community. Let us take a simple example. The whole experience of *Eretz Yisrael* as a state, and the widespread opposition to the State of Israel, is a covenantal experience. We cannot explain it in plain universal terms and categories. But the commitment of the Jew owes to its being the promised land. So the promise is the cause. But the cause is not some event in the past, the cause is the anticipation of something beautiful, something miraculous, something magnificent in the future—the fulfillment of the promise. The future actually generates Jews' commitment to *Eretz Yisrael*, even though it is a mad commitment.

In other words, the future is responsible for the present. Therefore the covenantal experience can be understood only in unique covenantal categories; universal forms of thought are inapplicable to covenantal events. The covenant created a new concept, the concept of destiny. This is what has determined the unfolding of Jewish history—not the departure point but the destination. The Jew is not a wanderer but an experienced traveler. There is a destination toward which he is rushing. That destination is the eschatological redemption not only of mankind but also of the world, of the universal consciousness.

Historical destiny can be characterized not only by teleology or destination but also by another feature. There is a contradiction in our historical experience, for there is no purely covenantal historical experience. The reason is obvious: Since the days of Abraham, Jews have lived among and dealt with non-Jews.

Modern Jews are integrated into gentile society in a hundred ways—economically, politically, culturally, socially. Since we live among gentiles, we share in the universal historical experience. The universal problems faced by humanity are also faced by the Jew. Famine, disease, war, oppression, materialism, atheism, permissiveness, pollution of the environment—all these are problems which history has imposed not only on the general community but also on the covenantal community. We have no right to tell mankind that these problems are exclusively theirs. God has charged man with the task of fighting evil, of subduing the destructive forces in nature and transforming them into constructive forces. The Jew is a member of humanity. God's command to "be fertile and multiply; fill the land and conquer it, dominate the fish of the sea, the birds of the sky, and every beast that walks the land" (Gen. 1:28) is addressed equally to non-Jew and Jew. As human beings, Jews are duty bound to contribute to the general welfare regardless of the treatment accorded them by society.

Rashi quotes a midrash which says that Hebron was called Kiryat Arba because four couples were buried there (Gen. 23:2). One couple was Adam and Eve; the other three were the patriarchs and matriarchs. They were buried in the same cave as Adam and Eve in order to demonstrate that there is no gap between universal human dignity and Jewish covenantal sanctity. Abraham did not appear in the arena of history to free the Jew from his historical human obligations, God forbid. The covenant, on the contrary, enhances and elevates the universal norms, adding many more prescriptions to those the Jew accepted as a human being before the covenant was forged.

There is no contradiction between laws that are rooted in the idea of *imago Dei*, the dignity of man, and those based upon the concept of *kedushah*, sanctity, which pertains to the covenantal community. The covenantal commitment creates an existential tension, because the Jew has a commitment which the non-Jew does not understand. Non-Jews would like the

Jews to have a general commitment to, and identify themselves with, their non-Jewish neighbors. But we repeat to them, to our friends and neighbors, the words Abraham addressed to the two lads: "Stay here, *poh*, with the ass, and I and the boy will go there, *koh*" (Gen. 22:5). In this brief sentence Abraham described in the most pointed manner the tension between Jew and non-Jew, between on the one hand, the two lads, who had a universal commitment, and on the other hand, himself and Isaac, who shared in the universal commitment but in addition had a covenantal commitment. The universal commitment he called *poh*; the covenantal commitment he called *koh*. Sometimes *koh* signifies "here," and sometimes it connotes *sham*, "there." Stand here and wait for me; we go there, we go beyond. The gentile does not understand the difference between *poh* and *koh*; thus the conflict between us and our neighbors is acute. But to experience this tension is precisely what it means to be an elected community, the descendants of Abraham.

❧ Index of Topics and Names

freedom
in confrontation with God, 88
and creative genius, 87
of decision, 35, 54
from environment, 20
through exile, 75
hedonic, 36-37
historical, 8-10
of man, 35-38
of the mind, 14
from slavery, 146-149
surrender of, 137, 188
of will, 94 100

G
Gad, 62
galut. See exile.
Gaon of Vilna. *See* Vilna Gaon.
Gehazi, 118
Genesis, 7, 12, 18, 90, 105
Gerar, 193
Gerizim, 64-65
Germany, 67, 120
gerut. See conversion.
gevurah, 15-16, 177, 193-194
Gog, 126
Goiim, 128
gomel. See birkat ha-gomel.
Gomorrah, 124, 127-128, 169
goral (fate), 87
Gospels, 180
gossip, 174, 199-200
Great Assembly, 174
Greek
emphasis on man's intellect
and spirit, 171
tragedy, 35
Gromer, Yaakov, 120

H
Hagar, 114, 200
Haggadah, 104, 155
Haggai, 32
hagirah, 73-74, 76-77
hakhnasat orehim (hospitality),

16-17, 168-169, 195-199
hakkarah (recognition), 29-31
Halakhah
Bet Shammai and Bet Hillel,
10
in cases of conflict between
two norms, 15
equates joy with the awareness of God's presence, 33
interferes with every phase of
human life, 181
logic of, 9
on *masorah*, 6
masters of, 120
on modesty, 171
prohibits theft from gentiles,
124
and the prophet, 100
on *sedeh miknah* and *sedeh
ahuzzah*, 153
on *shtar hithayvut*, 137
study of, 160
on *talmud Torah*, prayer, and
emunah, 188-193
translation of experience, 25-
34
on universal and covenantal
mission, 106
Hallel, 23, 33
Haman, 180
hamas, 124
Hamor, 64
Haran, 51-63, 114, 116-119, 151
hasidim rishonim, 175
Hasidism, 164
R. Hayyim of Volozhin, 174
Hazal
on Amraphel, 126
on continuity of tradition, 39
on the generation of the dispersion, 127
on God visiting Abraham, 167-
168
on Og, 129
on losing a *talmid*, 118

🍃 Index of Biblical and Rabbinic Sources